PRAISE FOR *BOSS VIBES*

"Nita Patel guides readers through a deliberate study of what it means to be both polite and personally effective. Her writing style is as informative as it is entertaining. A keen student of observation, she builds on her extensive personal experiences to highlight many fundamental yet overlooked standards of etiquette. Particularly valuable are her 'takeaways' where Patel summarizes key points in formats that can easily be retained and applied in everyday practice. All together, Patel weaves together a very helpful mosaic of rules, standards, and thoughtful tips that can help anyone present their best face to the world."

—**Chris P. Long, PhD,** Paul Naughton Associate Professor of Management, Director of Faculty Research, Director, Executive-in-Residence Program (EIRP), The Peter J. Tobin College of Business, St. John's University (NYC)

"In *Boss Vibes*, author Nita Patel proves you are the boss of you. It's a delightful, comprehensive guide to mindfulness, manners, and empowerment. This is a well-written and insightful read with common sense tips on branding the best in yourself. A must-read for all ages and for anyone who wants to succeed in both the business and social world. I highly recommend it."

—**Nancy Lombardo,** host of *What's The Buzz NY* on Blog Talk Radio

"Some people would argue politeness is not a virtue but merely a facade. Nita Patel masterfully shows us how to make the leap from simple actions of appreciation towards others to the development of one's moral character and civility. Here are nine principles to master for a great reward of increased confidence, strength, and satisfaction. Get your boss vibes going!"

—**Gabriela Pelin,** Blockchain Business Leader, IBM (Watson Health)

"Everyone will find this book an easy, but potent and useful approach to successful behavior in the workplace and at leisure. Its life lessons apply to every aspect of one's life. The concepts are sensible, effective, and a must for understanding how self-improvement will lead to a happier life. This book's content provides a framework to move from mediocre interactions with others to excellence in conversation and actions. *Boss Vibes* should be required reading for business owners, employees, teenagers, and people from every walk of life!"

—**Judith Fischer,** RJ ASSOCIATES

"Brash, timely, and necessary. Nita Patel writes an old-fashioned etiquette book for the 21st century. You'll present your best self at job interviews, on dates, and online. Follow Patel's gutsy advice—and don't forget to say thank you."

—**Adriane Berg,** Speaker, spokesperson, and host of Generation Bold Radio.com

"Nita's book, *Boss Vibes*, presents and explains in an easygoing, refreshing way why etiquette (custom, protocol, and propriety) is not a relic of the past, but is critically important in modern business life. She breaks down into atomic particles the elements of that old cliché, *You never get a second chance to make a first impression.* In sum, Nita explains why showing respect for others is good for business, as well as good for you!"

—**Rodney Hilton Brown, Esq.,** J.D., published author, collector, historian, speaker, and veteran of the cutthroat world of Wall Street investment banking

"*Boss Vibes* is a tell-it-like-it-is, no-holds-barred guide to etiquette in the 21st century. Whether you are a young career professional or still a teenager, *Boss Vibes* is a quick and easy read, with valuable insights for living your best life and moving upward and forward in your working life."

> —**Beth Rasin,** JD, Executive counsel to businesses and non-profits, and career strategist for young graduates

"A must-read book."

> —**Carolyn Barth,** CEO, Digital Content Strategy LLC

"Now here is a book that you must add to your reading list! Nita Patel has written the definitive guide to taking your personal brand and your professional life to new heights of happiness, success, and achievement. This book is edgy, real, and very witty but is also filled with deeply wise and implementable practical gems. *Boss Vibes* takes you on a journey to build your self-esteem, so you can operate at your highest potential in every aspect of your life."

> —**Hiten Bhatt,** International speaker and author of
> *The Leadership Adventure*

BOSS VIBES

SELF-ESTEEM, SUCCESS, AND THE ART OF ETIQUETTE

NITA PATEL

RIVER GROVE
BOOKS

Published by River Grove Books
Austin, TX
www.rivergrovebooks.com

Distributed by River Grove Books

Design and composition by Greenleaf Book Group
Cover design by Greenleaf Book Group
"Fire Opal I" on cover by Nita Patel

Publisher's Cataloging-in-Publication data is available.

Print ISBN: 978-1-63299-303-8

eBook ISBN: 978-1-63299-304-5

First Edition

To my beautiful and challenging family—
and to all of yours.

CONTENTS

INTRODUCTION

IT'S ALL ABOUT YOU

Manners and Mindfulness for
Self-Confidence and Success

Picture a young girl sitting at the dinner table with her family. Her brother, about seven years old, does something that disgusts and offends her. Perhaps he belches loudly or speaks with his mouth full, sending particles of food toward her. "Don't you have any manners?" she snaps.

Her eyes practically pop out of her head when he responds, "Don't you have any girlers?" Shocked, she realizes he had no idea what she was even talking about. Apparently, he thinks manners have something to do with being a man versus a girl. It was a clever response, no matter how clueless.

As you may have guessed, I was that girl, already aware that there were rules of behavior, which were best followed. As I grew older, I also grew frustrated with the American education system not wanting to teach basic etiquette. While attending school in London for a short period, I experienced the significant difference in what was taught there compared with schooling in the States. Common life skills such as swimming and dancing were mandatory, as was instruction in what was "proper." When you're a kid with just enough Southern influence to result in "yeah" accidentally slipping out—only, now you get scolded for it—you learn very quickly what is appropriate and what's not. British teachers had far more freedom to discipline than their US counterparts, so no mistake slid by uncorrected. Being raised in a blend of cultures, I learned a lot about why people do what they do.

After spending twenty years in the corporate world, I grew even more irritated. Very common mannerisms irked me. They still do, not because they're abominable or deeply insulting, but because I believe that simply as a human being, you deserve to respect yourself and be respected by others. Over and over again, I see men and women, young and old, regardless of where they're from, what they do for a living, or where they went to school, commit errors that would have given my proper London schoolmarms the vapors.

So, here I am, hoping to be of help by offering some easy, basic steps that will result in a more refined you. This new version of you will not only be polished and respected but will be a you bursting with confidence and self-esteem. You are probably reading this right now because you have come to realize or suspect that the time has come to brush up on your etiquette IQ. Perhaps you've wondered why everyone else seems to catch breaks and want to see if there's something you're lacking that holds you back. Perhaps, like a pesky older sister, someone has chided you by asking, "Don't you have any manners?" Or maybe you've noted the politeness of others and seen that these people exude strength, satisfaction, and an aura of success. It's easy to underestimate the results and not grasp the benefits until you actually put the basic rules of politeness into practice, but once you do, you will experience those results personally. These Boss Vibes will allow you to be your best self.

As I was researching what guidance on common etiquette was currently available, I was surprised to find the most well-known books to be dated, while recent articles seemed to be about not using your cell phone during dinner or not staring at it while attending important meetings or when conversing with others. *Too narrow,* I thought. *No wonder so many people seem rude or thoughtless these days.* When the pure basics—what we once referred to as *common etiquette*—are no longer recognized, it's time for society to realize how crucial the small things are. Once you do, they don't seem small at all.

"YOUR ACTIONS ARE YOUR ONLY TRUE BELONGINGS."
—ALLAN LOKOS

What are manners? And if your parents taught you etiquette when you were a kid, why brush up on it now? For starters, manners today are not necessarily the same as those you were taught as a child. Manners evolve with the times. Not too long ago it was unacceptable to call someone older by their first name. A relaxation of strict rules is always welcome, but that doesn't require throwing the rules of civilization into the dumpster to just hang loose. Nor are good manners simply a tool for humoring people or sucking up to bosses or your girlfriend's mother; good manners are the key to greater self-esteem, which leads to success in business and satisfaction in life.

The word "etiquette" comes from the French word for "ticket," which is fitting, because proper manners have always been our ticket to ride. Wherever you want to go, good manners will smooth the path to getting you there as they help you become the best you can be. They are part of your brand.

Today we're all about personal branding and showing people who we are. Instagram and other such social media have made authenticity practically a fetish, but showing people your authenticity doesn't mean ignoring boundaries. Society continues to run on rules, and following those rules is a brand enhancer. Each of us needs to understand the importance of respecting both ourselves and others if we want our brand to be noted with approval. Behaving in the best manner and showing consideration toward others—even if they don't notice it—increases our self-respect, which in turn feeds our confidence and self-esteem.

You might wonder why you should take advice from me or even listen to me at all. To keep it simple, I've studied people professionally, and spent the last twenty-five years helping them. From my collective experience I can tell you how people can make a great impression as opposed to just getting by. I have a formal education in psychology, and have taken several graduate-level management courses; I've hired and led large teams up to two hundred people; I've started a women's resource group, where I've coached executive women to feel confident and comfortable in front of crowds. And I myself have been on a stage since my early teen years through various activities, and have facilitated and spoken in front of audiences up to a thousand people.

Aside from that, I was the "cool mom" to my son's friends throughout high school and beyond, and I leveraged opportunities to teach them how to have a comfortable conversation with an adult at an age where everything feels awkward. Making eye contact can be daunting to a teenager, especially with an adult. Showing them simple techniques of body language helped them gain confidence immediately. Seeing their transformation inspired me to expand my audience to help teens and young adults in a formal setting through high school and university programs.

Working and interacting with many young people has made me aware that it's easy to get the wrong idea about what kind of behavior leads to fulfillment and success. We see obnoxious people get ahead and sometimes emulate them, not realizing that their triumphs aren't sustainable. Sustainable success comes to those who focus on personal growth and development, on improving themselves and not just their skills, who lend a hand to others rather than pushing past anyone who gets in their way.

Do you find networking events and encountering strangers intimidating? When your self-esteem is solidly backing you, you will always know how to approach new people and new conversations. Knowing your elevator speech and having an intention will boost your confidence in any setting. As long as you're putting your best foot forward, whether at a Meetup, a job interview, or on a date, you will get the best return on the time you put into the effort.

BEING THOUGHTFUL MEANS THINKING ABOUT YOUR EFFECT ON THE WORLD

There are two keys to good manners: mindfulness and common sense. We're all so busy these days that we sometimes lose awareness that, like us, other people are the center of their own universes. Being mindful of others encourages mindfulness in them as well. What do I mean by mindfulness? Think of it as acting with full awareness of how your actions affect and influence others and not intruding on their space in a way that might be offensive and off-putting. Mindfulness means being considerate and thoughtful toward all. Mindful people are always aware that their actions, whether kind or negative, will have ripple effects that impact others. In other words, being mindful means not wanting to lessen anyone's pleasure by doing something that could have been done differently. Once you start practicing mindfulness, it will become effortless and natural.

The second key to good manners is plain common sense. How many times a week on social media do we read something or see a photo and gasp, "What were they thinking?" Common sense should make you aware that what you wear to the gym isn't proper attire for a wedding or funeral. It should keep you from speaking so loudly that strangers can't tune out your conversation. It should make you aware that in any conversation, people should all be able to have their say. And, as my brother learned, it should drive home the point that you don't exist in a vacuum and should make an effort not to annoy, insult, or disgust others.

"POLITENESS AND CONSIDERATION FOR OTHERS IS LIKE
INVESTING PENNIES AND GETTING DOLLARS BACK."
—THOMAS SOWELL

I am here because I want to help. No one can "make" you do anything, but I hope you will think of the information I am going to provide as a blueprint, and that when all is said and done, it will bring you better relationships, more success in business, and more pride in who you are. And this is how Boss Vibes will lead to being your best self.

We'll take a look at every aspect of etiquette, not just in the old "mind your Ps and Qs" sense, but in terms of the meaning behind the manners: why it's better to do things this way than that, how behaving appropriately makes you a better person and improves the world around you, and why perfecting your brand will help you get ahead without sacrificing your authenticity or benefiting at the cost of someone else's loss. We'll take a look at every aspect of basic etiquette, including—

- How what you wear brands your image for better or worse

- The dual arts of conversation: talking *and* listening

- The basics of civilization and courtesy

- Keeping bothersome bodily habits from betraying you

- Tips to banish teenage angst

- Twenty-first-century restaurant rules

- Workplace wisdom to boost your career

- Building a public profile that will boost your personal confidence

- Taking your manners on the road

I hope to make you laugh, cringe, and most of all *think* about the things you do every day. It's easy and painless. Work with the blueprint and you will find that manners, once mastered, will be there every day to help you achieve your dreams and the admiration of others.

CHAPTER 1

SASSY OR CLASSY?

What Your Clothes and Style Say About You

Did you know that you don't have to open your mouth for people to judge you? In fact, you might not even have a chance to say a single word before others start to size you up. Studies show that first impressions are formed in as little as seven *seconds* of meeting someone. Simply seeing—according to some studies—is evaluating. As millennial expert Ashira Prossack puts it, "You've got a lot to pack into those seven seconds to make your impression a positive one."

If you're packing those seconds with the wrong attire, poor body language, or ghastly grooming, you might be lost before you get around to saying hello. So I'm here to help you clean up your act. Think of me as your personal shopper for this chapter—even though I'll be picking more items and shouting, "Do *not* wear this!" than filling your shopping bag with goodies.

"But I've got to be *me!*" you grumble. By all means, be yourself. That is, after all, the easiest self to be. But be your *best* self. That means developing a personal sense of style that's original and that hints at who you are as a person, but that is also always appropriate and never makes people want to close their eyes and run for cover like extras in a disaster movie.

Now, you may or may not know this, but it's true: Americans, in general, are more relaxed. If you travel the world, you can't help but notice that few people in other countries wake up and throw on yoga pants or running shorts without any intention of working out. In the United States, yoga pants and workout tops have become a cultural symbol of convenience. Instead, why not express your incredible sense of style, while also expressing a respect for the public realm that we all have to share?

One afternoon I walked into a conference room for my first in-person meeting with a rather senior consultant I had been working virtually with. He was from one of the top five most-reputable consulting firms in the world. I approached to shake his hand. However, before extending it, first he touched his nose. *Oh, no!* I was about to shake that hand and suddenly started calculating how quickly I could escape to re-sanitize. On top of that, as I reached my hand out, my eyes suddenly locked onto the fact that his fly was wide open and a bit of his shirttail was sticking out from it.

Of course, I tried to be discreet and not look as horrified as I felt while maintaining eye contact and sharing greetings. But I completely lost my train of thought! I was embarrassed, yes, but I also wanted to save *him* from further embarrassment. I felt like an extra in *Sharknado,* desperate to run for cover as Great Whites fell from the sky—except I wasn't allowed to flee! I had to stay there, engaged in polite conversation. How can anyone maintain their train of thought and focus on get-acquainted chitchat with *that* in front of their face?

And if men face a variety of potential wardrobe catastrophes, women have it worse. We have so many more possibilities of mishaps, if only because the immense variety of accessories available to us increases the odds. I once interviewed a beautiful young lady, probably in her mid-thirties. She was ambitious. She really wanted the job. But she blew it.

Now, it's true that if I met her at a party, I'd compliment her on her talent for accessorizing. But this wasn't a party. It was a job interview, during which all I could hear or see were her dangly earrings flapping back and forth with every move, her big rings clanking against one another as she talked with her hands, and her purple and gold nails sparkling in my face. I don't think I actually heard a thing she said, I was so dazed by the hypnotic power of those dancing earrings, percussive rings, and dazzling sparkles. I found myself wondering if she really knew what type of a job she was interviewing for. This was a pretty conservative company, and no one dressed like they were going to a holiday party. It was apparent that whether she was intellectually qualified or not, she would not fit in culturally. Needless to say, she did not get the job. Knowing how much she wanted it, I found it unfortunate that she had not come prepared to be taken seriously, and instead had focused on looking like the best dressed at a holiday party.

"You can have anything you want in life if you dress for it," is how the great Oscar-winning designer Edith Head put it.

Let that be your mantra.

WHAT IS WELL-DRESSED?

A sultry style might work to a woman's advantage when going on a date or even a girls' night out, but in other life situations, it often results in being snickered about or not taken seriously. And being laughed at might not only impede your career, it's also murder on your self-image and poison to your confidence. You'll never get to the top at work if they don't take you seriously—unless you're in a movie. But you're not. Life is not a movie.

It's quite simple. When we dress well, people around us cannot help but sense our confidence. If we dress like slobs, it signals that we don't care how we look—which means we don't respect ourselves. Others, whether consciously or not, pick up on that cue and treat us accordingly. From there it's easy to get stuck in a cycle of look-bad-feel-bad self-loathing. Whereas the opposite is also true: A great personal style announces a positive self-image and elicits positive feedback. It's what we all strive for, isn't it? It's why we seek validation from others, hoping they'll tell us how great we look today and how awesome our outfit is.

Remember, though, that looking stylish doesn't mean looking like a walking promotion for brand names, no matter how expensive. Sporting designer logos just to show you can afford them won't gain anything for you, unless you're a celebrity getting paid for endorsements. And just because you *can* afford designer brands doesn't mean it's classy to look like a NASCAR driver, covered in logos. Two at a time is more than enough. It's like getting your car gold-plated just because you have the cash to do it. It attracts attention, yes—because it's hideous. Endorse *yourself!* Why not create your own personal statement that screams—or, better yet, calmly states—*your* name, who *you* are?

"FASHION FADES. ONLY STYLE REMAINS THE SAME."
—COCO CHANEL

As for messages, who you don't want to be, if you ask me, is someone who is blaring political, social, cutesy, or defiant statements at the rest of the world. There are many ways to support your beliefs or causes without walking around daring people to disagree with the slogan plastered across your chest or on the back of your jacket. Besides usually striking others as just plain over-the-top, wearing this garb can also have repercussions, offending people and even egging on those who would like nothing better than to hurt those with your beliefs. Why not just volunteer or donate instead?

It's important to note that being age appropriate in how you dress never goes out of style. Age-*inappropriate* dressing comes in all sizes and genders but is most challenging for women, given the plentiful ways to dress and accessorize. For men, it's much simpler as they have a top and a bottom, which is typically some form of pants or shorts. The important thing to note is dress for the setting you're in.

Boss Vibes Style Standards: Know Your Numbers

In your 20s: Take advantage of the wear-anything-and-make-it-seem-trendy years, but sweats and hoodies do *not* go with everything.

In your 30s: Toss those clubbing clothes; there's so much more style to explore.

In your 40s: Yoga pants and flapping shorts are meant for yoga or workouts. Leggings are meant for winter sports. Got that?

In your 50s: Donate heels too high and anything glittery, torn, or distressed. Anything above the knees is too short.

WHO CAN YOU TRUST?

The first person you should trust is you. Not you on your own, however. You with your mirror.

When you're all togged out and ready to hit the road, whether for work, play, the gym, the clubs, a special event, or just grocery shopping, stand in front of the mirror. And I don't mean the one on your medicine cabinet. I mean a good full-length mirror. If you can afford the cost and have the space, the kind they have in some clothing shops and dressing rooms is an invaluable possession you will never regret owning—that's the kind featuring two moveable hinged panels on the sides so you can check yourself out from every angle. And I do mean every angle.

Look into that mirror carefully, being as objective as possible in considering how you look, then try to put yourself in the place of other people. What would your mother say? Your significant other? Your most trusted friend? Your boss? If the answer is "Eeeek!" figure out why. If you have doubts, take a selfie and send an SOS to that trusted friend. This will help keep you from being inappropriately dressed for a cocktail party or being judged by moms at a PTA meeting.

As you survey yourself from top to toe, ask, *Would I go to meet my future in-laws or show up for an important meeting or job interview looking like this and expect to be treated seriously and with respect? Does my hair look like I just got out of bed? Does my makeup scream "bargain bin"? Is this jacket too "Hey, man, that's a decade ago"?*

Not only is bedhead vastly unattractive, it also reminds people that you were recently *in bed*, not necessarily someplace they would like to picture you (or you would like them to picture you). Other thoughts are sure to follow: *Has he brushed his teeth? Did she bathe?* If you don't have a three-way mirror, check the back of your head with a hand mirror. And speaking of beds, pajamas are not acceptable for wearing in public unless you're at a hospital. Or if you're under three feet tall and holding a teddy bear.

Meanwhile, back at the mirror, it's never a bad idea to get a glimpse of yourself sitting down. Just pull a chair over or keep a folding one nearby. If you can see your underwear when you're standing or sitting, you're doing it wrong. Ladies, if you're wearing a very short dress and the only reason your panties don't show when you sit down is because you're not wearing any, get thee to a nunnery! Seriously, don't show any wares you aren't selling. The same goes for bras. I don't care how alluring you think that black lace bra is, keep it under your clothing. And the trashy trend of wearing bras beneath sheer tops? Madonna did that decades ago, so stop thinking you're cutting-edge and leave it in the '80s. Men, whether you're in boxers, briefs, bikinis, a G-string, or a jockstrap, no one wants to see any of those hiked up out of the waistband of your pants. If you want to show off your manly underwear in public, bulk up and become Magic Mike. Take my word for it: When it comes to flaunting undergarments, you're just badly dressed unless you're on tour hawking a song or video. Remember, you are not Lady Gaga or Childish Gambino. The prefix "under" is there for a reason.

Let's keep all parts personal and private covered appropriately. Being aware of how certain garments fit you is important.

There is one person *never* to trust if you want to know how good an outfit looks on you, and that is a salesperson. A salesperson isn't really there to advise, help you shop, or serve your best interests. A salesperson is there to sell. Yes, some salespeople will say, "Oh, that's not really for you," but few will do so until you've already expressed some dissatisfaction.

Now, before you leave that mirror, check to make sure you haven't succumbed to the kiss of death for appropriate dressing, which is always Too Tight. I know most of you would probably agree wholeheartedly with this and say, "Oh, I'd never wear something that was too tight." I also know some of you have to lie flat on the bed or the floor to zip up your pants. Being able to breathe is far more important than being able to fit into a certain size, which no one will ever know or see. And remember, if you're struggling to breathe in an outfit, how can you possibly enjoy yourself?

Don't leave this to chance. Here's how you'll know if your dress or pants or body-fitting shirt is too tight. Is breathing an effort unless you take shallow breaths like someone about to hyperventilate? Does any part of your body hurt when you sit or walk? Are any of your body's creases or crevices perfectly defined on the exterior of your apparel? Ladies, is that a back bulge we see behind you? Guys, do you think anyone wants to nibble that muffin top? Please keep in mind that just because something is your size doesn't mean it's your style. Sharply tapered designer shirts were not designed with heavier men in mind. Nor is Qiana or any other clingy fabric fit for a body with bulges or cellulite, because those flaws will stand out as clearly as if you were naked. Please don't forget, especially you men, that there's also such a thing as too loose. Baggy, falling-down sweats are just fine for a Friday night Netflix binge-watch party on your couch. Outside of that, you just look like someone who's undergone sudden weight loss and haven't bought clothes that fit the new you.

Two final reminders. First, regardless of how good you look, don't miss the sniff test before donning any garments, unless they were washed or dry-cleaned recently. Too many attractively dressed people ruin a fine first impression the instant they get closer. Body odor isn't sweet, while a blend of BO and stale dry-cleaning fluid is nauseating. And the musty smell of dirty clothes pulled out of the laundry basket can be downright deadly . . . to a budding romance or a promising career. Second, lint belongs in one place only, and that is the wastebasket. I suggest having both a large lint roller and a velour-type lint brush in your closet and keeping a small, travel-sized roller in your bag, briefcase, or car. In a pinch, you can ask a receptionist, salesperson, or restaurant server for a piece of clear tape about six inches long, insert one end between your pinkie and ring finger and the other between your middle and index finger, and tap away. This is helpful when dining out anywhere classy enough to have cloth napkins. Speaking of which, don't hesitate to ask for a black napkin, because the white ones tend to deposit masses of dust and lint on any piece of black clothing.

HOW TO DRESS RIGHT EVERY TIME

It's not all that hard to avoid showing up looking like you're going to a masquerade rather than a wedding or a job interview. Do some research if it's a special occasion. Call around and see what your friends will be wearing. Going to a new restaurant? Look up the website and see if it has photos of patrons or mentions a dress code. Think about the job you're interviewing for—not just the position itself but the company's image. Is it a hip, happening social media start-up, a dry-as-dust private bank, a sharp-and-slick hedge fund? Dress the part. Birthday party, wedding, funeral? Remember that you're there to either celebrate or pay respect to the guest of honor, not to draw attention to yourself. No one has the right to upstage the guest of honor or the bride or groom. That's an unfailing rule of thumb.

You will have much less risk of dressing disasters if you go through your closet and eliminate the stuff that's passé, age inappropriate, or the wrong size. After all, your old fabulous could be someone else's treasure. So, get yours out there where someone can use them. Your closet needs to breathe! Something you've kept for ten years is not "vintage." It is simply "old." A sweater boasting almost as many fuzzies as fuzz-free areas is not appropriate and has got to go. When a garment looks like you pulled it out of the dirty clothes hamper even after it's been washed and ironed, give it the boot. If you're too lazy to iron, stop trying to talk yourself into believing that un-ironed cotton or linen is a thing. It may *be* a thing, but it is not a thing of beauty. If your closet is so jam-packed you can barely pull out a shirt or pair of pants without everything around it tagging along, it's time to declutter. If you've been hanging on to something because "it will look great once I've lost twenty pounds" and the pounds are hanging on, show it the door.

My personal rule of closet—if I haven't worn it in the past twelve months, it has to go. Period!

And now let's talk about shoes, because shoes say a lot about a person. You can have on a great suit and then you get to the shoes and—what happened? Remember, it is the details that allow you to stand apart from the crowd. Small details make a huge difference. Clean, polished shoes are the bare minimum. If you're actually baring your toes, whether you're a man or a woman, please be sure your hygiene and grooming are optimal. No one wants to look at dirty feet in need of a pedicure.

Nowadays there's a lot of flexibility when it comes to shoes, though for a job interview, sandals are best left at home. Men wear sneakers with suits, and women don't feel forced to wear heels anymore. There are so many elegant flats and low heels available today that you can save the stilettos for after dark. If you do choose to wear high heels, it's your responsibility to learn to walk elegantly in them. Walking in heels is natural for some women but a learned skill for others. The whole point of heels is to enhance your feminine side. Have you seen a cat walk? Not at New York Fashion Week—I mean like a cheetah in the wild. You can feel the prowess, authority, and impeccable beauty in the way she walks and carries herself. If wearing your heels doesn't make you feel either powerful or like a princess, you might want to reassess the type of heels you're wearing.

You might also want to learn to walk taller and with confidence, carrying your weight in your core rather than clumping along flat-footed while torturing your beautifully pedicured feet with all your body weight, but that's for a later discussion. Plodding along or tottering like a child playing dress-up makes the wearer look silly. When that wearer is you, you won't want to end up tripping, falling, losing a shoe, or breaking a heel. Even the most graceful among us isn't immune—Naomi Campbell, for instance, hasn't lived down the awkward tumble she took on a Fashion Week runway thanks to some absurdly sky-high platform shoes.

Your footwear can be eye-catching, but your walk should be unobtrusive. I was recently at a Prada store trying on a pair of sling-back heels. As I walked around the store in a shoe one size too big, the salesman said, "Your shoes should never make a flapping sound like that when you walk." He refused to allow me to buy them even though I loved the shoe, and he missed an opportunity to sell. Not only was he being true to his beliefs, he was also sharing his wisdom on style and elegance. His statement showed that not *all* salespeople are just out to close the deal. Those are words to live by—for men as well. Learn to walk with grace; do not slog along unless sporting army boots. And finally, if your shoes squeak, take them to a shoe repair and get them to quiet down.

Keep in mind what the king of shoe designers, Christian Louboutin, said, "Shoes transform your body language and attitude. They lift you physically and emotionally."

It isn't just your shoes that define you. It's everything you wear. When in doubt about what clothing, shoes, or accessories fit different occasions, here are some simple suggestions of what will work for almost any of them.

Women

- Black pants or pencil skirt, with a simple blouse, dressier if the occasion demands it. For the latter, silk or chiffon is best, but nowadays, polyester fabrics can be beautiful and look elegant. A white cotton shirt can be universally dressed up or down with just the right accessories. Knit tops or sweaters are fine for the office or more casual outings. Heels or flats are equally acceptable.

- The little black dress is a legend for a very good reason: It can always be dressed up or down. It fits almost any occasion, other than super-casual or sporty events.

- Dark jeans (indigo or black) paired with a blouse or tunic are fine for most outings. Wear with dressy or nonsporty shoes, which could be heels, flats, wedges, boots, or low platforms.

- A dress with heels, boots, or flats.

- The key to dressing up your outfit is a belt, scarf, cuff bracelet, or a statement necklace.

- To dress down an outfit, you can add a cotton scarf, sneakers, or a hat.

- Steer clear of big, dangly earrings, as they can be a huge distraction for any occasion where your visual communication is key to the appointment or event.

Men

- Trousers, including denim, in any dark color with a shirt of any color, preferably tucked in with trousers but not necessary with jeans. Shoe and belt choice can dress this up or down for almost any occasion.

- Dark jeans (indigo or black) paired with a well-pressed T-shirt, Henley, or polo shirt and topped with a casual jacket or blazer.

We'll discuss your personal grooming later in the book (consider getting a manicure and pedicure in the meantime—yes, men, too). Right now, I want to call your attention to something people notice immediately, even before they scan the details of your outfit. I am talking about your posture, the bearing of that

body on which you'll be displaying your appropriate new ward-
robe wherever you go.

DON'T BE A SLUMPY SCHLUMP

Your mother was right: Stand up straight! Your posture is very
much a part of your style. Someone with head down, shoulders
sloping forward, shuffling along, or slouching in a chair while
bent over a cell phone or computer always looks like someone
without much self-confidence. James Dean has been dead over
half a century, the Beatniks are as extinct as the woolly mammoths
they often resembled, and poor posture was always overrated as
the height of cool anyhow. The taller you stand or sit, the better
you'll feel. If you are slouched over as you read this now, sit up
straight and tall and see how much better you feel, not just phys-
ically but mentally. Straightening your back is also contagious.
Next time you find yourself slouching in a room full of people,
roll your shoulders back and stand up tall, and then watch how
many others around you will adjust their posture.

Posture when sitting includes what you do with those
sometimes-pesky appendages, your legs. In my opinion, it's not
okay for a woman to sit with her legs wide open, no matter what
she's wearing. I use the term woman because a lady would never
sit that way. There's something charming and graceful about
the way a woman looks when she crosses her legs at the ankle
and slightly back to one side. (At the knee is acceptable if your
skirt isn't too short.) Since you're reading this book, I imagine
it's for self-improvement, so this is a way to improve yourself
and the impression you make. You could be the smartest person
in the room, the most fashion-forward woman at a party or

the savviest at a business meeting, but the moment you're seen with your legs open, regardless of what you're wearing, you'll be showing your lack of respect—for others and, worse, yourself—even if not actually flaunting areas not meant to be displayed in public. If you don't respect yourself, you lose clout. That's just how it is.

Men, too, should snap those legs closed. Manspreading is so common it's now a term, and it has yet to be used positively. That wide stance isn't sexy, and looks more intended to intimidate than turn anyone on. So just stop. It doesn't make you look like the powerful hunk of manhood you might think. It just makes you look uncouth.

Remember that scene in *Identity Theft* where Melissa McCarthy steals a dress, goes to the salon, has her hair and makeup done (stealing a few more products along the way), and suddenly feels like such a different human being that despite her previous behavior, even her rival Jason Bateman sees her differently when she shows up for dinner? I'm not telling you to steal clothes. All I'm saying is, "Own it!" Own how you put yourself together, and the world will see you as you desire.

Not only will you project self-confidence if you follow these rules, you will also *become* more confident and at ease with yourself. You can do it. You can be classy for free. No need to shell out hundreds of dollars or even more on an outfit. We all know cash and class don't necessarily go hand in hand. Far from it!

You might think you have the self-confidence act down pat, but the truth is that self-confidence comes across differently when it's real versus when you're faking it. Start right now. The next time you go out choose your clothes with care, stand in front of the mirror, and run down your checklist. Then put your chin up, your shoulders back, and walk out the door into the first of a lifetime of great days! After all, "Fashion is not something that exists in dresses only. Fashion is in the sky, in the street, fashion has to do with ideas, the way we live, what is happening." Coco Chanel said that, and if she wasn't the authority on fashion, *nobody* is!

CHAPTER 2

TONGUE TWISTERS

Surviving Conversational Quicksand

When I was young, I used to think I was the only girl in the world who got embarrassed by her parents. They just talked so loudly anytime we were out in public. You know how it is when you're a teenager—you're mortified by anything that might make other people give you or your family the side-eye. My mom was no help at all. Anytime I tried to shush her, she'd shrug it off, saying (loudly, of course), "So what? Who cares?" And my parents' voices would grow louder and louder as my face got redder and redder.

Nowadays, that same volume level, voices as loud as those that embarrassed me so much years ago, are, sadly, the norm. I'm not talking about the occasional "I'm so excited!" or "I'm expressing myself" kind of loudness. I'm talking about straight-up blaring your thoughts out as if you were a loudspeaker, using an outdoor voice that could serve to shout out to someone across a field, and filling in perfect strangers on details about your life that should be kept *entre nous*, between you and the person you're addressing.

I recently flew back from a trip to Paris and, while cultural differences are always obvious when I travel, this lady on my flight took them to new heights. After landing at the Dallas airport, the planeload of us waited at the bag carousel for our luggage. Suddenly this woman began projecting loudly as though onstage, although what she was on was her phone. She told her friend she needed a drink, that she wanted to meet within the next two hours (yes, after a 10½-hour flight), how her cat would probably reject her when she got home, and what a relief it was to be speaking English again. She then screeched a broken French phrase in her strong Texan accent. My son, who was traveling with me, leaned over and said softly, "I wonder if she realizes she probably doesn't need another drink." Everyone was trying to act as if they weren't hearing the conversation yet making faces that showed we were all in sync about the whole awkward situation.

Inappropriately loud is always *too* loud.

This woman was proof that you can be inappropriately loud without even having another person present in the conversation—we are often surrounded by annoying folks FaceTiming or otherwise speakerphoning in public. You see them everywhere: at the supermarket sharing intimate details with everyone in the checkout line; bellowing poolside where people are attempting to read and otherwise pass a peaceful respite in the sun; on trains and planes; on crowded elevators; and at the movies during the trailers. The experience is even more maddening when the speakers are pacing rather than standing in place, because then there isn't a quiet place to be found. Instead, the sound surrounds you as a lingering echo that intensifies and fades constantly as the miscreant does laps.

We're all embarrassed by friends or family on occasion and we all have lapses when we realize we ourselves need to keep it down. But that mustn't fool us into thinking this is acceptable. If your parents do something that makes you grit your teeth, you can humor them, but you needn't decide it's okay and that you can just continue their legacy. Anyone who has dined at the home of a family of sustained shouters knows habits learned around the dinner table, like political loyalties, tend to be handed down through generations unless the chain is forcibly broken. You can break the chain without offending your parents—simply by not following their lead. Everyone wants to rebel against their parents, right? This is an easy way to do that!

As far as conversation goes, I'd like to share some rules you might not be aware of, and some that will help you make a better impression—and keep you from embarrassing yourself.

YOUR VOICE: MUSICAL INSTRUMENT OR INSTRUMENT OF TORTURE?

You have probably heard your own voice in a recording; most of us have. But have you ever listened to yourself objectively? Try recording yourself twice on your cell phone: first, speaking into the phone as if someone asked you a question, or reading a response you have prepared, then recording a bit of an actual, unpracticed conversation you're having with someone. Don't cringe or be overly judgmental, but listen to both, paying attention to—

- The sound of your voice: Is it pleasing to the ear, not braying or squeaky, not too high or low in pitch? You can change the tone of your voice with exercises, many of them easy to find online. Your voice should remind people of a violin or cello solo, not chalk on a blackboard or sandpaper on wood. Remember, an annoying voice reduces the impact of the words and makes it harder for the listener to pay attention.

- Your volume: Do you notice that you are MUCH LOUDER speaking to someone else than when you practice on your own? That isn't uncommon, and it's a good thing to remember in conversation. How can you tell if you're piling on the decibels? Listeners will lean away from you, while a quick look around will usually show you that those nearby who are not a part of your conversation are suddenly engaged in what you're saying. Also, if you even *think* you're being too loud, you're probably right. Few people speak too softly, other than those with sore throats or the painfully shy. It's easy to tell, in a noisy room, for example, that you should speak up if the people you're talking to squint as if straining to hear, lean closer with knitted brows, or ask you to repeat yourself. One of the most important rules of communication in general, and especially in the workplace, is Be Aware. The communal break room is for taking a break and relaxing, not for being forced to listen to Amanda's boyfriend problem or Brett's run-in with his manager. And in the modern office, with its shared work tables and cubicles, loud talking is more than an annoyance—it affects productivity for everyone, not just you.

ARE YOU A GOOD SPEAKER?

It isn't just your voice that counts. There's a reason conversation is called an art. When you enter into discourse with any person or people, you are entering into an agreement involving respect. The purpose of conversation is communication: passing on or gaining information and ideas, exchanging views or experiences. Good communication consists of mutual understanding and being understood, not annoying the listener or airing your pet peeves. Accomplishing the job of conversing in an appropriate and time-effective manner involves attending to—

- Your responsibility: Every conversation, short of talking to yourself in the mirror, involves a shared responsibility. All parties are expected to listen, not speak over anyone else, not interrupt, not mumble, and make eye contact. Eye contact is too often forgotten, but I'm sure, like me, you have often given up on having a decent conversation with someone who isn't looking at you but is checking their phone or scoping out the room. Eye contact is a key to making others feel recognized and respected when they speak, as are empathetic signs, such as nodding, that you are fully involved and listening as opposed to thinking about what *you* will say next. Making supportive or "co-signing" sounds is actually distracting. It's best to remain quiet and respond in a supportive way versus feeling the need to make noise. Remember, being a good talker will never surpass being a great listener. Good listening also includes asking questions, which not only shows the speaker you're paying attention but can keep the conversation going into new areas. If you want to be the best listener possible, check out a study conducted by Jack Zenger and Joseph Folkman, the focus of their article "How to Be a Better Listener" in the *Harvard Business Review*, July 2014.

- Your introductions: You have a responsibility to introduce people if you are the person the others have in common. For example, if you're speaking to someone at a party or an event and someone else you know comes up, you should introduce them. If you happen to be the host of a party, you must act the role of a host, which means introducing people to others and adding something they have in common. Intros along the lines of "Nancy, I'd like you to meet Joan. She loves cooking (*Deadpool*, marathons, whatever) as much as you do!" are what help get a party warmed up.

"MOST PEOPLE DO NOT LISTEN WITH THE INTENT TO UNDERSTAND; THEY LISTEN WITH THE INTENT TO REPLY."
—STEPHEN R. COVEY

- Your words: Unless speaking with good friends you know will be comfortable with swearing, don't be a potty mouth. We all know a lot of #*@&%s and such are being thrown around in conversation these days as well as in most of the films that aren't for kiddies. This doesn't mean profanity is necessary (it isn't) or acceptable, and it could have the opposite effect you strive for, causing people you would like to impress with your hipness to see you as a no-class low-life. Look at it this way: bleepable words rarely add a single thing to any conversation—that's why they can be bleeped without leaving TV watchers clueless as to what the sentence was about. Curse words do nothing but put negative energy into the air. Someone who doesn't use them never looks less cool or less worldly than others. Nor do they strike others as puritanical—because people simply *don't notice* when you don't use bad language, only when you *do*. Unless you have the talent of Samuel Jackson, hurling expletives into sentences just sounds lazy, thoughtless, and poorly educated. Leave it to those getting paid big bucks on the big screen.

- Your vocal tics: Almost everyone has one or two, but by working on them, we can limit them. Why do that? Because they distract people, and your point may not be received—and even if it is, you've probably made yourself seem weak, so you won't be persuasive. Do you tend to use inflections as if asking a question? Do you state your name like it's a question versus a firm response? "My name is Sarah?" versus "My name is Sarah." You might even have a look on your face as if requesting approval of your own name. Other tics include peppering your remarks with "um," "like," "you know," or slurring your words in the vocal equivalent of slouching. This impacts both your confidence and how others see you.

- Your endearments: Guess what, hon? Many other cultures have long viewed Americans as too casual. Many foreigners, especially in business, still can't believe we start right in calling people by their first names. In almost all other countries, it is still the rule rather than the exception to address older people, and even younger ones in places like banks and government offices, by their title and last name unless asked to be more familiar. Not in the United States, where not only do most people, even in business, go for your first name right away, they'll even shorten it! If you're Michael, they'll call you Mike or Mikey; if you're Susan, they're fine with dubbing you Susie or Sue, never caring that many Davids cringe at Dave, and a multitude of Patricias writhe at Patsy or Pat. And first names aren't the end of it, because even in the most offhand interactions, people—especially people under thirty—start throwing around endearments as if they were confetti at a parade. Mingle enough, go shopping, stop for a drink or a bite to eat, and chances are you will be called one of the following more than once: sweetie, hon, doll, babe, dude, man, buddy, my friend, sugar. This is especially ludicrous if you're a fortysomething being addressed by a twentysomething whose sweetie you would never dream of being. However, depending on what part of the country you're from, the rules may vary. The key here is to be aware of your surroundings to ensure you're not offending someone.

WORDLESS COMMUNICATION

It isn't necessary to speak to communicate, of course. Nonverbal communication or body language is as important as your voice or your words. I've already mentioned some forms of this—for example, eye contact, leaning in, and nodding. I've conducted trainings on body language, so I know it isn't something we consciously think about most of the time. But again, awareness is the key.

Conversations often include personal space. Unless at a business meeting or interview, where seats are assigned, most of your conversations involve choices when seated or standing.

Do you stand too close? If people back away from you when you're speaking to them, it doesn't necessarily mean you have bad breath. You might just have invaded their personal space, a tactic that is intimidating even if neither of you consciously realizes it. You can't define precisely what personal space is; you just need to be aware of it.

One reason personal space isn't easily defined is that it changes depending on the genders of the people conversing, the nature of the relationship, ages, and so on. But a solid rule of thumb would be that it ranges from a foot and half for friends and family members to approximately three or four feet for strangers or VIPs, with a measurement in the midrange for coworkers and immediate superiors.

The same rule applies while seated: Do not get too close. If you are motioned to a chair next to your boss's desk, sit in the chair exactly where it is. Don't move it closer. When you lean in during a conversation, advance far enough to look super-attentive but not so far that you could be mistaken as aggressive.

> "WHAT YOU DO SPEAKS SO LOUD THAT
> I CANNOT HEAR WHAT YOU SAY."
> —RALPH WALDO EMERSON

Touching is certainly a hot workplace topic these days, and in that environment, the rule is clear: Simply do not touch people you don't know, or people at work, unless it's to shake hands, or if the latter are close personal friends. Never touch people to get their attention. You can make a point without grabbing someone's forearm and say goodbye without hugs or backslapping. By all means, keep your hands off people's children or pets unless you ask permission. It's not for you to decide that it's cool to rumple the hair of a stranger's child or cuddle their dog—and keep in mind that either one could bite you!

Your eyes alone can establish trust. Use eye contact to your benefit when in conversation. Give the speaker your full attention. The line between attentive eye contact and a staring contest is a fine one, so rather than locking eyes, try looking at your notes or your water bottle or somewhere else now and then, but not so often you seem bored and restless. A good rule of thumb is 60/70. A speaker usually leans toward 60 percent, while the listener typically leans toward 70 percent. Look away briefly without making the other person wonder if you're searching for someone more interesting to talk to or wondering when you can escape the conversation.

Body language used consciously can empower you in any situation. Listen with your whole body. Keep your toes and torso facing the person speaking, also known as "fronting." It allows you to appear focused and engaged. Fidgeting during a conversation conveys discomfort, weakness, or impatience, none of which is a good look.

A posture known for gaining immediate confidence can be achieved by locking your hands behind your head and elevating your legs, crossed at the ankle if you're sitting at a desk. Do this when you're alone, to pump up your confidence. If you're seated sans desk, the same feeling of confidence can be achieved by stretching your legs out and crossing them at the ankle while putting your hands in the above-mentioned position. Another confidence pose is making a fist and throwing it in the air as if you've just achieved victory. Again, these are private poses for making yourself more confident. They'll also boost your feelings when you're on the phone with someone, but not during a video call. Ann Cuddy, psychologist and author of *Presence: Bringing Your Boldest Self to Your Biggest Challenges* (Little, Brown and Company), says that people who stretch with their hands in an open "V" above their heads when they wake up are happier than others.

If you are an Amy Schumer fan, notice in *I Feel Pretty* (2018) how many times she throws her fists in the air when she's in fully confident versus self-pity mode. When she's feeling sorry for herself, she's curled up in a ball. This is a chicken-or-egg scenario. Do you want to feel confident? Experiment with various poses to see how it changes your emotional state almost immediately.

DEALING WITH DISCOMFORT

One of the most difficult etiquette situations is how to handle people whose bad manners disturb or unsettle you without either being rude yourself or asking for trouble. It's delicate, but you can do it. For instance, what can you do about aggressive fronting— when someone keeps inching closer as an intimidation ploy? You might want to give the space invader a quick kick, but that is rarely a good idea. If you have long hair, you can casually swish your hair as if unaware they're too close. Even if you don't manage to swat them with your tresses, they will usually get the idea when they realize their own space has been invaded. It can also help to cross your arms. This physically isolates you and makes it clear you aren't open to any invitation or intimidation.

This is an example of proxemics, the study of the human use of space and the effects that population density has on behavior, communication, and social interaction. In this chapter we have covered a few aspects of proxemics. When someone invades your space, it can also help to look at them and think of a lab rat whose behavior you're studying.

What if you're cornered by a bore (or boor) at a party or conference? You are allowed to bend the truth here. Just say, interrupting if necessary, something like, "Wow, that is so incredible/fascinating/unusual. I'm sorry not to hear more, but I need to meet my client to discuss business. Good to meet you!" You can say the last sentence as you're already walking away.

Personal questions? Asking them is not only downright presumptuous and uncouth, it's also a pet peeve of mine. I have heard everyone from thirtysomethings to young children expecting others to tell them things that are none of their business. Asking anything personal means asking a question that is inappropriate, regardless of who is asking and who is being asked. Period. It's like asking a lady or a gentleman their age. In today's ageist workplace, there is good reason never to tell people your age, and it's not only rude to ask someone, it could endanger their chances of promotion or even their employment in general. It has also been taboo to talk about money for many generations. That's why most people did not learn how to manage their finances until much later in life. Money management wasn't something typically taught to children by their parents. Kids who were patiently taught how to drive, cook, throw a ball, or raise a dog almost never learned their household income, expenses, and how to reconcile the two.

Obviously, some people have their own reasons for never wanting to discuss money. For instance, bosses often tell employees never to discuss merit increases or salary ranges because they don't want lower-paid employees to become disgruntled. Similarly, during job interviews, it's a battle royale, as both sides try to get the other to name a salary. (The rule of thumb here is that as the prospective employee, you should hang tight and try to force the employer to state the salary or a range so you won't embarrass yourself by asking for too much, or lowball and be stuck waiting a year or two to get the salary you wanted.)

This is less true in other countries, where salaries are discussed openly and even posted by job grade level. Not so in the US, where bandying about salary figures is frowned upon, so we end up without a sound grasp of our worth in the marketplace and of our overall financial situation.

Paradoxically, what we have ended up with is kids inappropriately asking each other how much everything costs. Let me just say that discussing money is very healthy. But as in all things, moderation is key. And that means you should never ask anyone how much their shoes cost or what their current salary is—and especially not in front of a crowd. If you're really interested in knowing the cost of something, there's always Google. Imagine if every time you walked into a meeting at the office someone asked you how much your suit cost. You'd probably hesitate to respond, as you don't want to appear either arrogant or cheap. But, more importantly, you'd be thinking of how ill-mannered this person was to ask such a question in public.

As far as conversations in general, I'm afraid I have no solid advice for handling the shouters. In a movie theater or other entertainment events, I would lean over and ask politely if they would mind not speaking to each other during the performance. At a restaurant, I suggest quietly asking the server or management to deliver the request, since the venue has a responsibility to all its customers. But shouters on cell phones are best ignored, the reason being that either they're in denial about being loudmouths or they just plain don't care about the comfort of others. In either case, they're likely to become belligerent and increase your displeasure without any resolution. It is sad indeed, but sometimes you just have to grin and bear it and get on with your life.

Boss Vibes Never-Nevers

- Never put your cell phone down in front of you when you sit down at a dinner table, and keep your ringer off in meetings, unless you apologize and excuse it as a matter of urgency on the order of "My mother is in the hospital and we're waiting for some results" or "I'm expecting a text about an important call to Tokyo."

- At a convention or anywhere else where name tags are worn, always admit if you can't remember someone's name rather than trying to read it awkwardly off a badge fastened on a man's or woman's chest or dangling from a lanyard. Regardless of where the badge might be, by the way, it is never a secret that you are reading.

- The right time for personal questions, whether it is to acquaintances ("Do you and your boyfriend live together?") or to someone in business ("Have you been looking for a better job?") is never. And it's always rude to ask about money, whether how much a friend pays in rent or how much a coworker makes in salary. This old rule is also a good rule: Someone else's religious or political views are their business, not yours.

- Don't brag. You can list your accomplishments or tell someone about recognition or success without appearing arrogant about it. As a rule, people prefer the humble to the big talker, the soft-seller to the shark.

- Be as clear as you are in speaking when sending text messages or emails. Don't take it for granted that everyone else speaks in emojis or hashtags. Unless you are communicating with best buds, use words and sentences. They never go out of style.

- Do shake hands when you meet someone new, with a handshake that is firm yet not bone-crushing. And please, please, please, don't hug people when you're introduced. Never never ever. You might think this makes you appear warm and open, but many others find it the creepy stuff of nightmares.

- Never talk down to anyone. Making someone else feel stupid won't make you look smart, just like a bully. The same goes for being argumentative. Conversations aren't about winning or losing. Those that are have a different name; they are debates, and both parties have signed on to that.

- Do use the name of the person once or twice in conversation, as this strengthens the connection between you, makes it clear in a group to whom you are speaking, and is an excellent technique for remembering people's names. Don't tag it onto every sentence, though. Avoid streams of words that run on the order of, "That's a great idea, John. You see, John, what we are trying to accomplish here is . . ." unless you want to see John's eyes glaze over.

COMMUNICATION IS YOUR MOST IMPORTANT ASSET

Nothing brings you success and popularity as dependably as your speech and conversational habits. We too often speak mindlessly, because we're too distracted, too casual. Life is not an ongoing party, a game show, or Casual Friday every day. Show your respect for others and they will respect you in turn.

The key will always be awareness and interest. Everyone in the world is interesting in some way. Train yourself to be a good listener, and you will find it easier to ask the right questions—and to be a good talker. All you need is genuine curiosity, good manners, and a pleasant and well-modulated voice, and you will sail smoothly on any conversational seas.

CHAPTER 3

BON APPÉTIT

Masterful Mastication and More

George Bernard Shaw once said, "There is no sincerer love than the love of food." No matter how much you love what is on your plate, you must never fail to treat it, and your dining companions, with respect.

We take much about our food for granted. We are no longer hunter-gatherers, so our food is easy to obtain—and to cook. And yet once seated at a table, many people approach their meal with boorish gracelessness.

Whether you live to eat or eat to live, dining today is an art, which can be easily mastered through some simple guidelines discussed in this chapter. Our utensils are as important to that art as the brush or chisel is to the artist. Hold them gracefully—never in a fist, but in the manner that you would hold a pen. The American style is to start with fork, tines down, in your left hand and knife in your right, cut a bite-sized piece of food, then put your knife down on your plate, move the fork to right hand, tines up, and eat the morsel. The Europeans don't make the switch. They hold the fork, tines down, in the left, cutting with the knife in the right, then bring the fork to the mouth. When not slicing, they keep the fork in the left hand, using the knife to push food onto it.

Neither method is more correct than the other. The main thing is not to be flicking bits at your neighbors, flipping food off your plate, or sloppily shoving it around. As an artist I'm always applying pressure to my thumb while holding a brush, and I've developed tendinitis in my right thumb that often makes it numb, so I avoid using the knife with my right hand as it could prove a hazard to anyone sitting next to me. Naturally, left-handers do the above in reverse, but you get the idea.

> ### "THE WORLD WAS MY OYSTER, BUT I USED THE WRONG FORK."
> —OSCAR WILDE

Unless you are a guest at a formal dinner, you will not have to keep track of highly involved multipiece place settings. Even salad forks are rarely seen these days. When in doubt, follow the old rule of using your utensils from the outside in, and the ones set horizontally at the top of your plate for dessert. There aren't too many silverware dos and don'ts—just a few sensible rules:

- Do not eat any food off a knife.

- No matter how exciting the conversation, do not wave any utensil while speaking. The proper movement is to put the spoon or fork down before speaking.

- When using a spoon to eat a liquid like soup or to ladle out a sauce, scoop away from yourself.

- Use your knife firmly, but do not broadly saw away at anything.

- If there are serving plates, don't use your own knife, spoon, or fork to take food when it is passed; always use the serving utensils.

- It's fine to use a large spoon to help twirl pasta onto your fork, but why not try just twirling it against your plate as Italians do?

- Always bring your fork or spoon to your mouth, never the opposite. In other words, soup should be carried carefully on your spoon from bowl to mouth. The same goes for peas or rice on your fork, even though it can be tricky. Bending over to get your mouth closer to the plate or bowl and ladling or shoveling the food in is a no-no.

- Speaking of silverware and your mouth, learn not to use your teeth when eating something off of a spoon. Your teeth are for biting and chewing, not removing soft material from a spoon.

- Don't attack butter with your knife. Cut off a flat square with your knife and put in on your dinner plate or bread plate, if you have the latter. If you are dining at a restaurant or someone's house and there are bread plates with a square of butter on them, just put enough butter on the knife each time to butter the small piece of roll or bread you have gently torn from the intact item on your plate and butter just that piece.

- If it's an Asian meal and chopsticks have been placed at your plate, do not rub them together before starting to eat; if they are the unfinished wood type, this is done to avoid splinters, but you are in little danger of getting splinters these days. If you are a guest and can't use chopsticks, just politely ask for silverware.

- When you're finished eating, put your knife and fork on your plate, parallel to each other, and your napkin, crumpled, next to your plate after the final course.

Anything you eat should be approached slowly and with grace. Don't slurp (unless you are eating ramen noodles in a Japanese restaurant, where it is expected) and don't gobble. Keep your mouth closed unless you wish to speak. Cut your food into small pieces. Cut those pieces one by one as you eat them. Do not cut an entire crèpe or omelet into pieces first and then eat them one by one; you're an adult.

Eating slowly doesn't just make the experience pleasant and more memorable, allowing you to savor each taste; it is actually better for your health. Research shows that the more you chew your food, the more easily it is digested, due to your salivary enzymes breaking down whatever you're eating. You will also be less likely to overeat, because it takes time for your body to register your fullness and send that signal to your brain. Bolting down a meal is what causes you to feel like a beached whale fifteen or twenty minutes after eating, when you find yourself moaning, "Oh, I ate too much!"

Keep those elbows off the table; that's the general rule. Some leeway is allowed between courses and once the meal is finished. As for your hands, you needn't make sure they're always in your lap, like a child at church, but they shouldn't be on the table, either. What is allowed is to rest one or both forearms gently on the table's edge, elbows bent and forearms perpendicular to your body, so your hand rests above the table rather than on it.

HANDS ACROSS THE TABLE

Your hands are vital to eating, of course, not just for using utensils, but also for putting your napkin in your lap, lifting it to gently pat your lips, and placing it on your chair (if you need to excuse yourself from the table for any reason) or next to your plate after eating. You need your hands for passing dishes—to the right, please—and for tearing off a piece of bread. You do not need your hands for reaching for anything not directly in front of you. If you need something from elsewhere on the table, ask that it be passed to you.

You will also need your hands for eating. One of the joys of life is eating with your hands—maybe because we're descended from humans who did, maybe because we're all kids at heart.

There are many foods you can eat with your hands. If you're not sure, you can wait to see what others do, or ask either your waiter or your host, depending on where you're dining.

These foods can be eaten with your fingers, for the most part—

- Any bread products, including rolls, biscuits, and muffins.

- Pizza—but if messy, eat with a knife and fork, as Europeans do.

- Artichokes—peel off the leaves one by one as you eat them. The heart can be eaten with the fingers, but I think that's messy and it's more easily eaten with a knife and fork.

- Most raw fruits.

- Hors d'oeuvres (the kind that can be passed) or snack foods such as chips and pretzels.

- Tacos, burritos, or nachos. Not enchiladas, as they're too drippy and gooey.

- Burgers and hot dogs in rolls.

- Any sandwich other than one with gravy.

- French fries, unless covered with any topping.

- Asparagus (if cold and with a dipping sauce).

Also, if you pick up any morsel from a communal plate or bowl, whether it is an olive, a cracker, or a small hors d'oeuvre, it is now yours and you don't get to decide you don't want it and put it back where it was. You eat it, or set it quietly on the side of your plate.

There are different rules for various ethnic foods, such as sushi and edamame in Japanese restaurants or Indian food eaten solely with bread as a utensil. But most of the time you'll find yourself eating those in a place where you can either observe others or ask someone what the rules are. Unless traveling abroad, you should not be confronted too many times with foods you haven't seen before. But if you are handed a plate with something you can't figure out how to eat—a pomegranate, cheese, or fruit fondue—just ask without any embarrassment. Don't be afraid to ask for help.

One thing that must never be in your hand at the table is a phone. It should not even be in sight.

And, while some food might be finger-lickin' good, don't be tempted to lick your fingers at the table. In fact, don't lick your fingers anywhere while eating anything. The most astonishing thing I've ever seen in my life was when out with a group of girlfriends who went to get ice cream after a dinner. As with most ice cream parlors, there weren't enough seats, and as usual it was freezing inside. So, we went outside to enjoy our dessert. As it was the middle of July, everyone's cone started dripping rather quickly. Some of the women had ice cream melting down to their fingers. But instead of using paper napkins to stanch the flow, two of the ladies started licking their fingers. At first, it didn't seem too strange. But then one girl switched hands and licked each of her fingers from top to bottom. I could not believe my eyes! I offered extra napkins. I also made sure my flavor sounded really boring, so no one would be interested in trying my ice cream with all their finger-lickin' activity. All I could think about was the gross things they may have touched between dinner and ice cream. All the door handles, the chair backs, their hair, their faces, a filthy cell phone screen, who knows what else?

BE A GOOD GUEST AND AN EXCELLENT HOST

It is important to learn how to be both an admirable guest and host, as being one is normally followed by being the other.

Be a good guest by generally minding your Ps and Qs. Stand until the older guests and host or hosts have taken their seats. Don't start eating before the host does—in olden days, doing so could have gotten you banished from any royal court. It is also polite to eat nothing until all at the table have filled their plates. Nowadays many might not notice, but it shows respect. Forget you brought a phone with you. Never take your phone out and set it on a dinner table when you are a guest. No one cares about the vitally important call you might be expecting. I realize mobile mindfulness has been mentioned already. However, as our cell phones have become a part of us, there are various aspects I'll continue to mention as they pertain to the topic.

Other don'ts as a guest are—

- Don't hog the wine or take extra-large portions of any passed dish.

- Don't even ask if you can smoke. Here is the answer: No.

- When you are invited, ask if you can bring something. If the answer is no, bring flowers, wine, or chocolates.

- Learn how to offer a prayer or blessing if you are asked. You can look up a nondenominational version or even one that avoids religion. You needn't be religious to be grateful for what you have.

- Learn how to make a toast. You can find instructions easily online, and it is always fitting to toast your host or hosts for the fine food and company.

- Sit in your chair and stay there. Do not rock your chair or move it to face someone you're speaking with. Don't leave your chair unless it's absolutely necessary, and excuse yourself if you need to. Don't announce where you're going. If the restroom location isn't known to you, stop at your host's chair and ask quietly.

- When eating at home, practice eating every meal without making noises: no slurps, gulps, or smacking. And never any belching. Compliment your host with words—"This pudding is delicious!"—but never with sounds, unless as a prelude, when it is all right to preface your remark with a gentle "Mm," as in "Mm, this is so good!"

"TABLE MANNERS ARE A SKILL THAT,
ONCE MASTERED, LASTS A LIFETIME."
—KATE SPADE

When you are playing the role of host, it is wise and polite to ask guests when they accept your invitation if there are foods they cannot eat (due to allergies or religious prohibitions). As a guest, if you are not asked (and nowadays, with everyone on different diets, it is a rare occasion not to be), make a point of informing your host of the same restrictions. Only mention a food you dislike if you absolutely could not swallow it and would embarrass yourself trying to get it down. Otherwise, be a good and adventurous guest, and eat whatever is put in front of you, at least a bite or two. You might find some new delicacies that will become old favorites!

Whether hosting a dinner or dining out with clients or friends, stay away from ordering anything messy or difficult to eat—certain sandwiches, for example, and certainly the burgers currently in vogue, the ones that stand six inches high and contain everything but the kitchen sink: short ribs, sour cream, guacamole, pickles, coleslaw. You should never end up with more of your food on the table, the floor, or your lap than in your stomach. A salad is always a good choice, easy to eat with just a fork and not likely to interrupt the flow of conversation as you wipe grease off your chin or stop to try to get your burger back into its roll.

Passing food and double-dipping with chips and dips and other wet foods is not only gauche, it's also a reliable way to catch the latest bug going around. The same goes for tasting others' drinks. If you offer anyone a taste of your food, do it before you have taken a bite, so you can cut off a piece with your knife and gently push it on their plate.

Always treat servers with respect when dining out; they work hard to make a living and take pride in what they do. If out with friends or business associates, don't order five courses if everyone else is having two, thereby making them wait and watch you eat until their own dishes come. And, whether at home or when dining out, never, ever scrape or stack plates or bowls at the table. This is a job that must always be relegated to kitchens.

When dining out, be aware of tipping customs, and ask for split checks if needed. If you're not up to date on tipping, you can read my advice for teens in chapter 6. It is the same for grown-ups.

Going back to the *Identity Theft* reference from chapter 1, just as Melissa McCarthy's character felt taller and more confident when she put on a pretty dress for dinner (at the end of her adventurous road trip), she was more sophisticated in her dining manners as well. If you watch the movie, note the way she holds the champagne glass just because she is in a nice restaurant, wearing her LBD. Compare that to how she acted at the diner earlier, eating with her hands and with manners that were completely the opposite. Why? Your environment makes a difference. I'm not saying it's okay to eat like a slob in the privacy of your home—just that when you create an experience around food, whether with flowers or candles at the dinner table, wearing something that makes you feel more attractive, or eating at a high-profile restaurant, your entire dining experience is elevated. You will naturally want to be more well-mannered and mindful about how you hold your glass or pick up a savory morsel. This food then makes a positive impact in your bloodstream. It's true, food is medicine. But how you eat it is medicinal.

Scientific research agrees with ancient Ayurveda, regarding the connection between your brain and tummy. When you are under extreme stress, your digestion is impacted in many ways. Similarly, when you eat from an emotionally balanced, joyous place, that food nourishes your physical body in ways no prescriptions can imitate. Your bloodstream can fully absorb the vitamins you're consuming when you eat from a joyous place of mind. This will also lead to you making better food choices.

The most important part of any meal is the pleasure of it, treating your food with the appreciation and respect a fine meal deserves, and relishing the company of those with whom you are dining. Do both, and you will have mastered the fine art of dining.

CHAPTER 4

PERSONAL AFFECTS

Keeping Your Bodily Habits Private

We all want others to like us, to find us good company, to consider us candidates for promotion at work, and to place us at the top of the list of desirable friends. And I've covered some of the areas vital to your success. But dressing right, speaking well, and mastering the basics of considerate manners are not all it takes. You might have those aspects of etiquette covered but still fall short in the search for career success and social esteem by committing one of various other social deal-breakers. Luckily, this is not a major challenge. It is something you can easily rise to and perfect as long as you are mindful and don't let your body intrude upon the niceties of congenial interaction.

Our bodies are wondrous things, amazing machines that function seemingly magically. Unfortunately, they are not perfect. They have drawbacks: Noxious odors get emitted, raucous sounds escape, things get stuck in our teeth, small but annoying masses clog our noses. We are not angels frolicking in a celestial rose garden but are all too human, a situation that can be both embarrassing and unpleasant. While this chapter, and the book in general, focuses on how to create your own brand of beauty, decorum, and self-respect through etiquette, there are some very basic topics that need to be discussed if you're to attain the desired level of grace and ensure that others find your company delightful.

Let's get one thing straight: While belching or passing gas may be part and parcel of being human, they are neither acceptable in public nor falling-down funny unless you are home alone or are ten years old. And caring for any part of your body—whether it is your fingernails or toenails, your teeth or your breakouts—is your personal business and should be conducted in private or with a trained professional, depending on what the problem is. Got that? Good, then let's get started.

NO ONE WANTS TO KNOW WHAT IS IN YOUR MOUTH

If this seems to be stating the obvious, let me just say that I have seen people to whom it is far from clear. I am talking about people who chew with their mouths open. There seem to be two basic styles of doing this—one, the standard grinding method, but openmouthed; the other, a sort of chomping style, in which the lower jaw descends straight down, then clamps shut, somewhat in the manner of a crocodile. Either of these modes treats all present to the sight of matter in various stages of mastication. While these are the styles of *habitual* openmouthed eaters, there is a third mode of which many of us are occasionally guilty. This happens when, at a party or even a business lunch, we get so involved in a conversation, so eager to get a clever line out or our opinion in, that we open our mouths in mid-chew and blurt it, often blurting bits of food as well. Don't do this. Remember what I said earlier and *be aware* that you need to curb your enthusiasm.

By the same token, you should never pick or floss your teeth in public. I would think this was a given—if I hadn't seen it done over and over again. Recently, I went to speak to someone at my workplace and found her standing at her desk flossing. I could actually spot particles flying out! In Europe, many restaurants put toothpicks on the table after a meal, which seems tacky, to say the least. But it's not unusual to see a party of four in, say, Italy sitting at the table enjoying an after-dinner espresso while all digging around with those picks! They're being polite about it, I suppose, because they always cover their mouths with one hand while holding the toothpick in the other, but it is still distracting and disgusting. Many restaurants in the US have a container of toothpicks by the front desk or, yes, even on the table. Do not be tempted. It's a good idea to carry a pick or some floss with you (or take one from that container), but there is a place for everything, and the place to do anything involving your teeth is the restroom.

Speaking of the restroom, the public sinks are not there for spitting in. If you like to rinse your mouth after eating, it's a good idea to carry a small bottle of water with you and do this in the privacy of a toilet stall. What if you're not spewing food or water around? You still should not work on your pearly whites in public. One of the most annoying things is people who use those little pointy rubber periodontal gum tools or woody sticks in public, with the excuse of "massaging" their gums. Massage away from me, please. No one wants to see any of this, because it's uncouth and inconsiderate.

In case it had never occurred to you, no one wants to know, or even think about, what's in your nose or lungs, either. This means do not pick your nose anywhere remotely in public, which includes while you're driving alone in your car. You do not become invisible behind the wheel. Also, don't think you can get away with it by pretending you're simply scratching your nose; we all know what you're doing. Blowing your nose should be done in the bathroom if possible. If it isn't possible, be discreet. This means that if you need to whip out a tissue because your nose has suddenly started running, just dab at it, then excuse yourself and go blow out your mucus in private. If you have no tissue, excuse yourself and get to a bathroom ASAP. Don't even think about wiping your nose on your sleeve. And, no matter how curious you might be, you never want to get caught examining the contents of your tissue or handkerchief. Trust me, you do not.

Spitting in public? Nope. It's disgusting even to spot a gob of phlegm lying on the sidewalk, much less watching someone hock it out. Let's not even get into how unsanitary this habit is.

Coughing and sneezing are often out of our control. If a sudden cough or sneeze arrives, direct it tightly into the crook of your elbow to avoid spreading germs. If you possibly can, do it elsewhere. If you're seized by a coughing spasm or feel one coming on, as long as you can ambulate, move away from others. What if you're under the weather and aren't able to stay home? If you have a cough or cold and need to go out, wear a mask. You can buy these at the drugstore, the disposable kind. (Note: If it hasn't occurred to you, good manners, in terms of consideration for others, is a good reason to get a flu shot even if you think you're naturally immune, as others are not.)

BETTER OUT THAN IN? I THINK NOT

I'm not at all sure why some people, usually men, consider saying "Better out than in" after belching or passing gas, as a statement that excuses them. It doesn't. Yes, these bodily functions are universal, but, no, they should not be performed in front of an audience. If you feel air bubbling through your large intestine, desperately seeking an escape, the proper response is to excuse yourself, tighten your butt cheeks, and go to the nearest private (and, if possible, ventilated) place. The same goes for suspecting your indigestion is ready to relieve itself with a hearty burp. Better in than out until you're on your own.

> "IT IS MY EXPERIENCE THAT WHEN PEOPLE
> SAY THEY ARE ONLY HUMAN, THEY HAVE BEEN
> MAKING BEASTS OF THEMSELVES."
> —THE MEAT INSPECTOR, IN *A PRIVATE FUNCTION*

And what if a noise or odor escapes in public from the temple that is your body before you can do anything about it? No, no, no—do not say, "Better out." There is only one thing to say, and that is, "Excuse me." If someone else is the guilty one and says "Excuse me," just smile, nod, and continue with whatever you were doing. Do *not* make a joke, even if you think it's well-meaning. Some who have had digestive cancers or other illnesses do find their systems occasionally emit noises or odors they can't help. Think how you would feel if you embarrassed them without meaning to.

The same reticence applies to blackheads and pimples. These should be saved for private squeezings and excavations in a place where no one else will be subjected to seeing anything popping out or being slowly extruded from your pore. This goes for other superficial removals, such as scabs, hangnails, and nose or chin hairs. Ditto for removal of "sleep," the debris that collects in the inner corners of the eyes. Women should check themselves during restroom visits for "shrimp eyes"—dark specks of shed mascara piling up in the corners of their eyes. Just keep it secret.

YOUR BITS AND PIECES

Oh my, there are so many body parts trying to sabotage us that at times it can be difficult to keep track! Men should never adjust their privates in public, period. Ladies will not be impressed or intimidated if you do. They will just think you're an ill-mannered oaf. The same goes for scratching those private parts. When you do, you look like a walking advertisement for scabies or body lice, and that is *not* attractive.

Your bits and pieces are called your "private parts" for a reason: because they should remain that way. That means no manspreading on subways or buses. In the office, it can be easily interpreted as harassment or intimidation. Ladies, you're not excused. Always keep your legs together, especially if you fancy wearing dresses.

Scratching anywhere in public is pretty much a no-no, unless it's a gentle brush at the tip of your nose or chin. Nor do we want to see bits and pieces of your nails flying hither and yon. This goes not only for clipping the nails of your fingers and toes (I recently read someone's complaint about a sandaled man clipping his toe-nails on an airplane!), but also for something as seemingly benign as filing your fingernails. You might have lovely fingernails, but no one wants your nail dust speckling their clothing. Nor do they enjoy watching anyone clipping their cuticles or, worse, biting them and spitting out the bits.

I have also noticed that some people are smellers. Not just those surreptitious armpit sniffers, but people who tend to massage their scalps or scratch their ears or maybe remove something from under a fingernail and sniff their fingers. I think this might be anxiety or compulsiveness, as they are often the same people who sniff their food before eating it, not in a savoring-the-aroma way but in an I-can't-help-it-I'm-a-sniffer manner. If this applies to you, please stop. Grace and beauty, remember?

Again, it would seem obvious to anyone with manners that this is a no-no, but I occasionally see people insert a finger in their ear, scrape it around, take it out, and examine what's under their nail before rolling the earwax into a ball and flicking it away. This is a transgression of the first degree. Keep it simple by not inserting things into body orifices in public, period, other than allowing a piece of silverware or a straw slide gracefully into your mouth in a restaurant. Also simple: anything that is in or part of your body is not meant to be seen, heard, or smelled, but rather is something that must remain private.

HAIRY CARE EEK!

I am not talking about the suicide method of hara-kiri, even though manners (or, rather, lack thereof) can lead to social suicide, but of the public care of your hair. Doing things with your hair in public—from constantly running your fingers through it, to brushing it, to tossing it here, there, and everywhere like a cheerleader's pompoms—is not appealing. Nor is the long-haired women's habit of publicly trimming their split ends (once again sending bits of themselves into our already-polluted environment). Can you imagine Charlize Theron on the red carpet at the Oscars, talking about her gown while constantly touching her hair to make sure it's beautiful and in place for the photographers awaiting her? Or what if politicians were tossing their hair habitually while discussing governmental policy? They are as much at work then as we are during our nine-to-five office hours—and fiddling with your hair or trying to be your own dermatologist doesn't belong in any workplace at any time.

Your eyebrows are hair as well. Public plucking is all right only if you're on a farm holding a dead chicken. And put that eyelash curler away! Applying any makeup in public is in bad taste. In an emergency, you can do a quick slash of lipstick or gloss at the table after dinner, but save the pencils, blushers, and anything that takes more than ten seconds for the restroom.

One other thing in the haircare category: no hairspray in public. In fact, I'm averse to using it (or spraying perfume) even in ladies' rooms, because so many are allergic to the products. You don't want to give people asthma attacks. If you use a spray or drop medication regularly—an inhaler, eyedrops, nasal spray—that application, too, should be performed out of the public eye.

Since we've been addressing things that should be done in restrooms, let's remember that no one wants to see what you've done there, either. Three things about that: flush, flush, and leave the sink clean. Men, put the toilet seat down. Women, if you're one of those whose mama taught her always to squat over any toilet seat outside her own home, check behind you before leaving the room to make sure everything went into the porcelain bowl designed for it. Any used feminine hygiene items should be deposited into the special receptacle located inside the stalls.

Boss Vibes Basics: Nita's List of Things to Do Diligently

1. Always flush.

2. Always wash your hands after using the restroom.

3. Don't leave a present for anyone, including yourself, in the sink: rinse after use.

4. Bathe daily.

5. Be aware of dandruff and wash your hair regularly. (The bedhead look is a clean, well-crafted style created with pleasantly scented hair products. Don't take it literally.)

6. Wear deodorant (or antiperspirant if you tend to get wet underarm marks on clothing).

7. Brush your teeth and hair at least twice daily.

8. Trim your nails (and cuticles if needed) bimonthly.

9. Don't forget to clean your ears.

10. Men, when you get a haircut, have your nose and ear hairs trimmed as well.

Yes, indeed, life would be easier for all of us if we didn't have to pop in and out of restrooms all the time, control ourselves, and clean up any mess we might otherwise be leaving behind. But our knowing when to do so makes every day much more civilized for us all. And that, of course, is exactly what manners are all about.

If you are a serial abuser of anything mentioned in this chapter, I suggest you also work at matching your private behavior as much as possible to what is acceptable in public. This will serve the purpose of increasing your mindfulness regarding habits that might offend. You will receive the added benefit of feeling quite elegant and refined.

CHAPTER 5

MICRO MOMENTS

Little Things Mean a Lot

"I look for pleasure in the details."
—ATOMIC BLONDE

Manners, like everything else in the world, change with time. Nowadays a man wearing a baseball cap is not expected to take it off in the presence of a woman, nor is he expected to stand when a woman gets up from the table. Even where the rules are concerned, we are more flexible than ever. Whereas bringing a wedding gift to the actual wedding rather than having it sent to the bride's home in advance was once considered a social gaffe, now everyone seems to do it. People even wear jeans and sweatshirts to funerals, much as I bemoan this casual lack of respect.

The main thing to be grasped in this chapter is that relaxed though we may be, the things your mother or grandmother taught you regarding garden-variety etiquette shouldn't be shrugged off.

Politeness will always be a virtue. It is, after all, what separates us from the new world of virtual assistants like Siri or Alexa. (I don't know about you, but Siri never thanks me, and lately she doesn't even give me answers, but just rattles off websites she expects me to look at on my own!) The small gestures will always be appreciated.

LITTLE THINGS DO MAKE A DIFFERENCE

When most people hear the word "etiquette," they tend to think of how a formal table setting should be arranged for dinner or which fork to use for which part of the meal. (We covered the basics of dining manners in chapter 3.) We so easily tend to forget the simple things, like smiling, saying thank you, or not letting a door slam in someone's face behind us. Life can be so hectic that people don't pay attention to things that make us human beings. Whether distracted by our phones, our worries, or the impending plans of our busy schedules, our attention often seems to be anywhere except present in the current moment. So while we can be relaxed about many of the old rules today, we must never toss the basics into the dustbin, if for no other reason than that they evolved to show respect, and are noted and appreciated—as their absence is noted and scorned.

Everyday etiquette starts with please, thank you, and you're welcome. These three expressions are not synonyms for "wouldja," "great," or "no worries."

I'm not sure when "no worries" was foisted upon us. It seems to be the mistaken current-day version of the Spanish "de nada" or the Italian "niente." But even in Spain and Italy, there are politer expressions such as "no hay de qué" or "con gusto" in Spanish and "prego" or "con piacere" in Italian.

"BE KIND WHENEVER POSSIBLE.
IT IS ALWAYS POSSIBLE."
—DALAI LAMA XIV

One of the simplest yet most valuable gestures you can make is to smile, yet so many people can't be bothered. We've all heard that a smile is contagious. You can spread good feelings just by smiling at people when you enter a store, a meeting, or almost any room at all. Smile at the next person you cross paths with. You never know when someone is having a horrible day and your simple smile can give them a gift of cheer in that moment. Or someone could be having an amazing day and that extra smile will amplify their joy. It's a good deed. Instant karma—you feel good the minute you share a genuine smile with someone. Smiles are not advisable when crossing paths with strangers on dark, empty streets at night or at most funerals (unless you have mastered the sad smile of condolence), but, otherwise, are always appropriate.

Some things that were done automatically at one time seem to have been forgotten or are ignored today. It would be nice to see them make a comeback, as they indicate not only respect for others but self-respect as well. For instance, saying thanks when you're given a gift. If you say it in person, it doesn't mean you shouldn't write a thank-you note as well, even if it arrives as an email or text message.

Two excellent phrases are "Excuse me" and "Pardon me." Use them when you bump into someone or when you're getting into a crowded elevator. It has now become the rule that we're expected to go to the rear of the elevator if we're headed to a farther floor or to the side if getting out sooner. But because something is expected doesn't make phrases of courtesy obsolete. The same goes for escalators: The British habit of standing to the right and passing on the left is now universal, but if the space is tight, you should excuse yourself rather than just shoving through.

CLOCKWISE: LATE IS NEVER GREAT

Being fashionably late is no longer a thing—if it ever really was. Sure, there are emergencies, such as accidents tying up traffic or not being able to get a cab, missing a train, and so on. But we all know perpetually late people. We all know how irritating it is. And we can't get these people to change unless we make sure that we are always on time ourselves. Lateness is rudeness. And it always will be. As well-put in an article on the website theartofmanliness.com, "Being late is stealing." Think about it. Would you steal money from someone's wallet or files from a business meeting when the other person isn't looking? If not, why would you steal their time?

There is one occasion when you have a slight time-buffer, some leniency regarding being punctual: at a party. A party does not mean a dinner, where people must never feel forced to wait for your arrival. But even at a large party, your buffer is limited. You do not have an open invitation to show up two hours late, especially if you compound that error by expecting everyone to hang on until the wee hours just to humor you. A good mantra for the perpetually late? Try, "It's not all about me." Being a guest has several requirements: making an effort to mingle and converse with people rather than looking upon the occasion as a free food and drink opportunity, arriving on time, and not overstaying your welcome.

Being prompt means leaving for your destination early enough to arrive on time. Pretty simple, really. It means not relying exclusively on navigation apps, which aren't always programmed to predict traffic accidents or sudden bursts of heavy traffic; not guesstimating that it will take about what it did three weeks ago on a different day at a different time, because every day or night isn't the same and certainly not weekend nights; and not ignoring the clock when you're getting ready so that you are late even before you leave.

If someone is picking you up to go somewhere, whether in their own car or in a taxi, be at the agreed-upon spot or ready to walk out the door *before* they arrive. That means being totally good to go short of grabbing a coat or jacket. What if there is a genuine crisis that makes you late? After all, these things happen. In the era of cell phones, there's no excuse for not calling or texting your host to say you're on the way but have been held up. It's the polite thing to do. Caveat: you are allowed to do this only rarely.

Late to work? Your lame excuses won't help anything. Your boss doesn't want to hear about your digestive problems or your pet's misbehavior, while statements like "I had to go back because I forgot to set the security alarm" or "I hit the snooze button, then overslept" just announce that you can't organize your life. I once had someone say, "I got to work in my trainers and discovered I'd forgotten to bring my dress shoes, so I needed to go back home to get them." I did not foresee a rapid career progression for this person.

If you're late joining a conference call or getting to a business meeting, just join it or take your seat, and keep quiet. Do not interrupt anyone else's conversation—or, worse, their presentation—with an apology. If you are not the guest of honor or leader of the meeting, wait to speak until it's your turn or you have worthwhile input. Women seem to apologize when walking in late far more than men do—in fact, women seem to apologize more in general. If you feel an apology is required, a simple "Sorry to be late" when opening your remarks will do. But don't apologize for every single thing in a business environment. Remember, the corporate world is filled with people reading books teaching them how to be sharks. Over-apologizing looks weak and can make *you* look like a shark's dinner.

What if you show up too early? You have two choices: You can pretend you did so on purpose, or you can go somewhere to kill time. The former works well only if it's a business meeting, when you can sit in an empty conference room on your computer and, if anyone asks you, just say you had some spare time so thought you would do some work on this or that project. Showing up half an hour or more in advance at anyone's house is just plain rude unless you're from the catering agency.

Being five or ten minutes early is negligible. However, being early as a habit is a sign you are doing something wrong: Perhaps you don't trust yourself to arrive on time. Learn to plan so you won't have wasted time by arriving too early or been rude by being late. If you simply like to be early, as some people do when traveling, not worrying about how long it will take to get through security and enjoying the ambiance of airports—as I am told some people do—that's fine. Oftentimes travelers who have TSA PreCheck plan to arrive at the airport closer to their boarding time, but always keep the unpredictable variables in mind, such as unforeseen traffic and security lines based on the day of the week and time of day.

If you focus on being aware of others' actions, it won't be hard for you to know for sure if you are always too early or too late (and I state this because so many people who are one or the other always tell me that they rarely are). Look at people's expressions. Do they appear surprised and not especially thrilled to find you the first to arrive? Do they raise their eyebrows and check their watches as they tear themselves away from other guests to welcome you? Listen to their words and their tone. "Oh! We weren't expecting anyone yet. I'm afraid we aren't ready" or "Weren't we supposed to be meeting at half past seven? Did I get the time wrong?" are pretty obvious.

And for those who are unprepared for serial early arrivers or irritated by the thoughtlessness of constant latecomers, you can help us all by ceasing to smile wanly as you say, "That's all right." Far better to state firmly, "Please sit down and make yourself comfortable, but we have a few things left to do on our own" or "Just so you know for next time, I wait for latecomers only ten minutes and then . . . (Insert 'I leave' or 'the meeting is closed'.)"

No one wants their personal brand, the "me" that we're sharing with the world, to be "I'm always late." It's like advertising "I'm not thoughtful" or "I'm unprofessional/undependable/disorganized."

And to give a little spiritual advice here, being late creates a very negative vibration. It sets the wrong idea in motion and you suddenly attract low-vibe scenarios—every traffic light is red, there's an accident right in front of you, traffic doesn't seem to be flowing. If you've watched the movie or read the book *The Secret*, it talks about how one negative thing creates a domino effect of negative things. Running late, hitting red lights, maybe having an accident—next thing you know, five other things have gone wrong all in that "being late" moment you were fighting your way out of. At a stoplight, you look at your email and discover your bank messed up on an auto-payment. Your boss has sent an email about how you didn't communicate the appropriate status on something, asking questions about what you already shared with her. Suddenly you start cursing at people on the road who have done nothing wrong. Whereas if you were on time and blasting your music with your happy face or dance moves, that same driver you were irritated at would be of no concern to you at all. Notice how, when on time, you're in control of your emotions. Late, and you let circumstance control them. So let's just leave it at this: Don't fight the laws of the universe.

CHIVALRY: NOT JUST FOR KNIGHTS ANYMORE

In this era of peak feminism, when women are furthering themselves in their careers and breaking the glass ceiling, chivalry is a topic of controversy. I hope I can make it less so. Let's start by going back to what chivalry is—or was in days of yore: gallant, courteous, generous behavior. Today, being chivalrous is defined as being courteous and gallant. Being courteous without asking for anything in return. While chivalry as a code of conduct does come from another era—one of knights and ladies, an era that is long gone—nowadays we can all be chivalrous to one another.

When a man opens a door for you or helps you with your coat, as a woman you needn't be offended nor, as another man, must you start worrying you look like Methuselah. Someone is just being polite. No one is thinking you're the weaker gender or somebody not capable of opening a door without assistance.

It is simply good manners and thoughtfulness. And if you prefer to put on your jacket without someone holding it, or to pull out your own chair, there is no need for *you* to be rude. You just say, "Thank you, but it's easier for me if I do it myself." (Although, let's be honest, it's so much easier when someone holds your jacket just right, so you can hold the edges of your cuffs and slip through the sleeves of your jacket without getting your shirt all wadded up at the elbow.) Thoughtfulness is a gift and we should show gratitude in the moment when we receive a gift. Life gives us presents all day long if we acknowledge them.

As the saying goes, you must give to receive. Call it karma or whatever else you like, the fact remains that when you give, you receive. Just as smiles are free, so is someone holding your coat for you—unless, of course, that someone is a hatcheck girl or guy, in which case they expect a tip, but, hey, the tip is for checking your coat and not for helping you put it on, so go ahead and enjoy it. As for whether men should continue to hold chairs, offer arms when crossing streets, assist with jackets, or rise to their feet when someone enters the room, that is their choice—although they're certainly all fitting and considerate gestures. The bottom line is that even if you're a twentysomething woman and a man in his thirties is holding a chair for you, you can sit or not sit, but you need not be offended or act it. Not everything needs to be about independence or self-sufficiency. Sometimes, we can just appreciate another human being's thoughtfulness and show our appreciation without anyone's feathers being ruffled.

As we go deeper into specific situations where manners are too often sadly lacking today, we will come up against topics your mother never told you about. But the topics we just discussed beautifully illustrate being gallant, courteous, and generous without asking for anything in return. With good manners, we can all be knights.

CHAPTER 6

HEY, TEENS!

Simple Steps Lead to Greatness

We all want to be liked and accepted, and I know this is especially important for teenagers like yourself. We are all different, all unique, and all motivated by our own reasons. Some people want to fit in, some want to lead the way, and still others enjoy their own individuality. But as human beings, we all need love, appreciation, and validation.

I have a teenager of my own, so I understand that the desire to be considered cool can outweigh everything else. But being cool won't count for much if you're crude, crass, and uncouth. It's not just parents and teachers who think that. If you make a list of the best-liked kids at school, I think you'll be holding a list of people who are thoughtful, polite, and considerate—without making a big deal of it.

You can elevate your image starting right now. What do I mean by that? I mean you can gain more respect from your friends (and your parents and teachers as well). You won't lose points by being a nicer, more gracious person. And you will end up feeling better about yourself. Why? Because thoughtful people become nicer and more confident people, and that means they have terrific self-esteem without being conceited.

Here are a few starter tips on things to do and not do to build your confidence.

- **Shake hands firmly.** This is a secret way of letting the other person know how you feel about yourself. But don't be a finger-crusher.

- **Make eye contact when you talk to someone.** This shows that you're confident, and, equally important, interested in what the other person is saying.

- **Stand tall and with your chin parallel to the floor rather than buried in your neck!** People want to see your eyes, not the top of your head. You don't need to throw back your shoulders like a soldier at dress parade, but you will feel more worthy of the things you want in life if you stand up straight and tall. When you slouch, you will both look and feel sloppy and unsure of yourself—not to mention the fact that it completely changes the way you feel about yourself when you stand tall. Try it out with a quick posture adjustment and add a smile for fun.

- **Work on the art of making conversation.** Find a website that lists trending topics. If you're on social media, you'll find trends on Twitter, Instagram, Snapchat, Facebook, or any of your favorite sites.

- **Appreciate others, showing them your respect and gratitude.** Congratulate them on making the swim team, acing a test, or getting their driver's license. If your skateboard gets away from you and someone picks it up and hands it to you (or even just nudges it over), if someone compliments you on your clothes or your hair, if a friend offers a ride home, be sure to thank them. The more you express your appreciation, the more you'll notice how nice people are around you.

- **Don't interrupt others—or worse, shout over them.** Think how frustrating that is when people do it to you.

- **Mood should not dictate your manners.** You just learned how to feel better instantly, but if that doesn't change your overall mood, it shouldn't impact how you behave toward others. While most people think the world should understand and accept a poor attitude from someone who's having a bad day, bad week, or bad year, there are no excuses for mistreating others due to your own self-pity.

In conversation, you can make an effort to be more mindful of what you say. For instance, you can make sure your language isn't hurtful to others. Using labels or stereotypes to refer to other people can be very hurtful, even if your intention was to set up the plot for sharing the story of something that happened to you. It's never good to use any words that could be considered hateful. If you're not sure what I mean, you can go online and look up "ableist" or "bigoted language." None of those words and phrases belong in a thinking, caring person's vocabulary.

Speaking of speaking, and of words and phrases: swearing doesn't make anyone cool. It just shows that they're too lazy to learn new words. That's one reason why it's useful to learn new words. Not only will that help you express yourself better, but as you start doing that, you'll sound smarter—both because you'll *be* smarter, and because you won't be saying "uh" and "like" so much.

We all have interesting things happen to us: some are good, some are bad, and some just make good stories to share with others. Exaggerating won't make them any better; it will just make it sound as if you made things up. Nor does embellishing a funny real-life incident make the anecdote any better. No one wants to be known as a drama queen.

DATING DOS AND DON'TS

When you go out on a date, whether it's your first date or your fifteenth, make an effort. Wear clean clothes, shower first, wash and dry your hair. If you're driving, get out of the car, go to the front door, but never pull up at the curb and honk the horn. Be polite to your date's parents. Shake hands and make small talk. You could admire the lawn or a painting in the living room, or talk about the weather. It's the thought, not the content, that counts.

If you're the person being picked up, be patient. Just smile pleasantly while they talk, then—if they are being awkward or enough conversation has been made—say politely, "Excuse me, but we should get going."

If you are doing the asking and you are going to a movie, plan to pay for both tickets. But if your date wants to buy their own, accept their wish politely. You can always say something like, "All right, but I'm paying for the drinks and popcorn." If you invited someone to dinner, play the host. Make sure you have checked out the restaurant online, so you know you can afford it. Make a reservation if it's a spot that takes them and be prepared to pay. If you're paying, make sure you have brought enough cash in the event your date orders the most expensive thing on the menu. If you're going with another couple or couples, consider asking for separate paired checks so you needn't do all the math involved in splitting the check. Plan to tip a minimum of 15 percent, up to 20 percent if the server was fantastic or you had extra-complicated orders or took up the table for a long period on a busy night. Figure on a dollar fifty to two on every ten dollars. Keep the math simple enough so you can look at a round figure of thirty dollars and immediately know that 20 percent would be six dollars. If you're one of those people who needs to tip the exact amount, I recommend discreetly using the calculator on your phone to do the math.

Here are a few other ideas for getting "restaurant ready" if you aren't used to dining out:

- Get some free chopsticks from an Asian restaurant and practice using them at home so you'll be prepared for Japanese or Chinese eateries.

- Your napkin belongs in your lap until you have finished, not on the table.

- Don't stack your plates. You might do so at home, but this is what servers are for.

- Look online for a list of foods that are okay to eat with your fingers in a restaurant. You can't go wrong if you use a knife and fork for pretty much everything other than burgers, sandwiches, corn on the cob, or anything meant to be dipped.

- Never snap your fingers at a server.
- Don't fold your napkin when you're finished. Simply crumple it and leave it next to your plate. Not on top of your plate, but next to it.

Most of all, try to enjoy yourself and do what you can so that your date enjoys the evening, too. Follow my suggestions and, trust me, you'll gain cool points.

DRESSING LIKE THE STARS

You might want nothing more than to dress like your favorite rapper or runway model, but it's not practical to try. What they wear is often purposely intended to shock (i.e., clickbait), chosen by a paid fashion stylist, or worn as part of a known or secret endorsement deal. Unless you, too, want to be an actor or musician, you might be better off simply appreciating their talent and persona rather than trying to copy their style. If it isn't you, don't wear it. Lady Gaga usually dresses just like everyone else when she isn't performing, at a high-profile public event, or appearing on a talk show.

And, girls, you'll be better off spending some of your makeup money on products that care for rather than cover your skin and clog your pores. Makeup is fun and glamorous, but all the stars you love wear that makeup for their public image. When they aren't actually working or doing PR, they prefer a natural look in makeup as well as clothing. Not only that, but their skin needs it! One of the biggest problems for young singers, actresses, and models is bad skin—slathering on the makeup all the time brings on breakouts, so they need to give their bodies' largest organ time to breathe and heal. As for those photos you see when they are working, they have either sat for several hours of preparation by professionals or been photoshopped to look perfect. Far better to allow your personal hygiene and attractive but nonshowbiz wardrobe to show off your self-respect and beauty than to smother it in fake lashes, painted-on brows, and layers of heavy foundation.

Speaking of hygiene, clean up your act before any date by washing your hair, showering, and brushing your teeth. Cleanliness should be an everyday thing for you: at least one shower or bath a day, washing your face in the morning and at night, and brushing and flossing your teeth. Wear the right size of clothing, not too big and baggy or too tight and clingy. And keep your shoes clean, too, instead of letting them look as if you just waded through a pile of trash. For all leathers, one of those insta-shine sponges with clear polish is all you need. For suede, you can buy a special sponge or brush in shoe repair shops.

Don't wear dirty clothes, on a date or any other time. And never try to cover up the musty smell of old clothes by spraying on cologne or aftershave. The added ingredient makes the bad smell worse. Much worse.

LEAVE THAT PHONE ALONE

You might be too young to clearly remember a world without the smartphones and tablets that now can accompany you anywhere. It was a world in which people paid more attention to the scenery around them and to the people they were actually sitting with. It was a world in which people did things like thinking and making decisions without checking out their phones at the same time. For real! As for our world today, studies show that smartphones can make people dumber and lonelier.

An article on aish.com discusses a 2017 study from the University of California in San Diego in which students taking tests to measure their cognitive ability were divided into three groups: the first had to leave their smartphones checked in the lobby before entering the testing area; the second could bring their phones with them but had to leave them in their pocket or purse; the third couldn't look at their phones but were allowed to put them on their desks. The lobby group not only performed best, they did significantly better than those who kept their phones out of sight. The worst group was those whose phones were on their desks, even though they said they hadn't even been thinking about them. The conclusion: just having your phone near you is a distraction that keeps you from learning or participating fully.

Other studies cited in the same article delved into how smartphones make you lose your ability to concentrate, think independently, and take part in conversations with ease. Sadly, with some teens sending over a hundred texts per day, overuse of smartphones is making many feel lonelier rather than connected, because they have fewer voice calls or face-to-face conversations.

I won't even go into the negative health effects of gaming for hours on end or poring over websites. Much has already been written on the effects of electronics on the ability to sleep and on vision. So, unless you have a specific photo you want to show people, keep your phone to yourself and out of sight when you're on a date or with friends or family.

BE A GOOD SPORT AND A GOOD CITIZEN

Good sportsmanship is one of the keys to being respected, liked, and successful, both in and out of school. Your behavior should be considerate of others, whether you're playing a board game with your little sister, a friendly game of cards or charades with your parents, or a basketball game. All these rules apply to both girls and boys. Being a good sport is never being weak or babyish. If you don't agree, look at the top athletes you admire. The best thing about being a good sport is that it is so easy to do!

First of all, it is important to show respect to everyone on and around the playing field or the rink or the court: friends, fans, the opposition, coaches, referees. Second, mind your manners on the field. Sure, it's a competition, but that doesn't excuse being mean-spirited. That means following the rules: no pushing or shoving in team sports (apart, maybe, from ice hockey), no being rude in games with others. Not only do you not want to be pushy when playing, you also don't want to be a hog—that means not hogging the ball or the spotlight. Often, the MVP isn't the showiest or the one who scores most, but the person most respected and admired by others.

Finally, always be both a good loser and a good winner.

A good loser congratulates the winning side and apologizes to their own team if they think they had anything to do with the win not being theirs. A good loser shows appreciation to their coaches and to the other team for playing well. That means recognizing others and not making excuses for yourself—and never blaming anyone for the loss or displaying anger.

A good winner pretty much acts the same way, with one important difference. A good winner never gloats or mocks their losing opponent. One of the most important lessons you will ever learn is this: being liked and respected is much more rewarding than acting like an arrogant winner. Games were designed to be enjoyed.

DON'T BE A LITERAL MALL RAT

You might be a mall rat who loves hanging at the mall, but that doesn't mean you should ever act like a rat, indifferent to the enjoyment of others. A mall is a place of business, not a playground. Shouting, running, and any kind of rowdy behavior isn't just annoying and disruptive in an enclosed area like a mall. It can be dangerous to the elderly and those with health problems. You can make it a better experience for everyone by, as the saying goes, acting your age and not your shoe size.

That means letting seniors go before you on escalators and elevators, and holding the doors open at shops. It's also cool to make sure you throw your trash into the proper receptacle. Treat public restrooms as if they were at your house and your mom would scold you if you didn't leave them as you found them.

Your behavior inside any store in the mall should also be considerate. Don't cut in line or throw clothes you don't want on the floor of dressing rooms. In fact, don't leave anything in a dressing room; either put it on the rack many shops have available just outside the try-on rooms themselves or leave it at the cashier's desk, telling them the clothes didn't work out. Always say thank you when leaving a store and treat the clerks politely. They have to deal with a lot of rudeness in their line of work and will appreciate your courtesy.

There is one big *never* about malls, and it goes for all stores in general. Do not be tempted to shoplift, whether it is something you dearly want but can't afford or on a dare. Shoplifting is theft. If you're caught, not only will your unhappy parents be contacted, but you might also be charged with a crime. A juvenile record won't help you get ahead in the world—or, at least, not in any world you would want to be a part of.

FIND A CAUSE GREATER THAN YOURSELF

Do you give back to your community, to the world? It is so exciting to see teens across the US getting involved in causes that make them take pride in their work and feel good about themselves by helping others. One of the issues most in the news these days is our climate and how we protect it, and teens—and even preteens—have been working to raise awareness of these issues. The media, in turn, take note of them and their commitment.

What causes do you feel strongly about? Animal welfare? Your religion? Teens your own age and younger children with serious illnesses who need help getting medical care, or just want their biggest wish to come true? Older people who might remind of your grandparents, but are lonely shut-ins?

Most worthy causes need volunteers or fundraisers to lend a helping hand. You can visit people in hospitals and nursing homes or find a way to raise a little money for foundations like Make-A-Wish or the American Society for the Prevention of Cruelty to Animals. Or maybe you'd like to get friends and neighbors to sponsor you in a charity walkathon or other race. There are many opportunities. You can search online or ask your school guidance counselor for assistance in finding a good cause that will welcome you. You will provide a valuable service to others not as lucky as you are, while at the same time growing your self-respect and gaining experience. Your unselfishness will also provide the bonus of giving your college applications a boost when the time comes.

LAST BUT NEVER LEAST: DON'T BE OR IGNORE A BULLY

There have always been and will always be bullies. You don't want to be one. Sure, on TV, in movies, and even in real life, some bullying types are presented as strong or humorous. But the truth is that bullies are weak and harmful. Just as you should be mindful of not saying hurtful things, you should also be mindful of not bullying others or accepting that behavior in your friends. Whether it's laughing as a classmate rudely shoves aside smaller kids in the halls at school or ignoring the "mean girls" giggling and pointing at someone who doesn't have the same kind of trendy clothes they consider a must, turning your back on bullying helps it spread. Unless it's something physically or mentally abusive, you needn't report the bully, but you can let them know that what they are doing is wrong and will make them unlikeable. A person willing to do so shows they are much stronger and courageous than the bully.

> "POLITENESS IS A SIGN OF DIGNITY, NOT A
> SIGN OF SUBSERVIENCE."
> —THEODORE ROOSEVELT

As I said, I have a teenager of my own, so I know this isn't always an easy time for you. I know you want to be popular and fit in, sometimes even more than doing well at your studies. But your teenage years aren't a rehearsal for some later do-over. You won't be allowed to go back and repeat these years. Theodore Roosevelt knew that kindness and consideration lead to happiness and are a sign of strength. Manners will make you a better person and help you set an example that will make others better, happier people, too. Don't do the wrong things because you feel pressured or are too lazy to do things right the first time. Stay mindful and be confident. Be willing to rise above the crowd and become a role model instead of a follower. If you can do that, you will have made an excellent start in your journey to success.

CHAPTER 7

THE OFFICE BLUEPRINT

Your How-To Workplace Guide

Workplace etiquette is important no matter where you work or what type of work you do, unless you have that rare career in which you never interact with anyone at all (a job that might not actually exist). Even if you work from home in your pajamas, you interact in business, and while some of this chapter focuses on corporate environments, almost everything in it applies to any workplace.

My advice here is about etiquette being a ticket to success in your career, both in terms of everyday business decorum, and in terms of moral integrity. You have certainly heard the old saying, "Be nice to people on the way up. You'll meet them on the way down." The reason this is such a well-known statement lies in its truthfulness. If you're rude or backstabbing, stepping on others' toes to advance your position or status, you might advance, but you will have weakened your chances of staying up there—and those upon whose toes you have trodden or over whose shoulders you have climbed will indeed take pleasure in seeing you pass them on the downward journey. So, before we go over a few basic dos and don'ts, let's talk about getting ahead by being your best self. After all, that's what etiquette is truly about.

GETTING AHEAD GRACIOUSLY

Graciousness is the most elevated tier of etiquette—one that improves the world and embodies concern and respect for others. The more often you practice it, the more it will become a part of you. The most important aspect of workplace etiquette isn't limited to actions like refilling the paper in the printer—it's about making any workplace a better place. And it pays off, too. You will enhance your chances for success by genuinely spreading goodwill and not climbing to the top on the backs of others.

You don't need to become a full-time mentor in order to help others, nor is there anything to lose by treating employees less senior than you with the same respect others might reserve for their supervisors (it is, in fact, a sign of strength, not weakness, if you do so). Be friendly to new employees, helping them find their way around and introducing them. Being new can be daunting, so a bit of help and a friendly face are always appreciated. On the other hand, when asked to do something that isn't part of your job by an equal in the pecking order (that is, anyone whose role doesn't include giving you orders), you have a right to stand up for yourself. This is a tricky area, I know, and I personally understand and appreciate that it can be especially risky for women. But there is nothing wrong with smiling and saying, "Sure, I'm happy to help you out this time, Christian" or "I wish I could, Sara, but I'm tied up with my own work right now." Either way, you have let someone know that you are well aware they're taking advantage of your good nature. Habitually being someone's dumping ground for tasks they don't feel like doing themselves won't necessarily bring rewards anyhow. The title of Lois P. Frankel's book *Nice Girls Still Don't Get the Corner Office* is not an exaggeration. Being assertive yet polite shows leadership qualities and tells others you are not there to cover up for them.

> "NEVER LOOK DOWN ON ANYBODY UNLESS YOU'RE HELPING THEM UP."
> —JESSE JACKSON

Showing your respect for others means apologizing for being late to a meeting if it means others were kept waiting, or for any other mishaps. Always accept responsibility—without pointing the finger at someone else or sharing too much personal information. For example, if you're late to work, simply say you're sorry. Be wary of adding too much information, especially if that TMI is "I was out so late last night I'm not totally awake yet" or "The kids weren't ready to be dropped off for day care." Avoid saying anything that could mark you as a potentially problematic employee.

How do you get ahead besides performing your job duties well? For starters, always be prepared. That means keeping track of your accomplishments. Updating your resume regularly is a boon, even if you don't foresee yourself looking for a job in the near future. Why? Because it gives you a ready-made list of accomplishments that you can use for your performance review or when requesting a pay increase or promotion.

As for the proper etiquette when you ask for any kind of upgrade, whether it's in terms of position or salary, you should present your case and keep it simple.

1. Begin with a polite, positive statement: how grateful you are to your team, how much you value the company, etc.

2. Be prepared to state why you deserve the upgrade, as in, "I think I deserve this (raise, promotion, benefit) because . . . " Make that statement as a prelude to enumerating your accomplishments.

3. Don't brag or cast aspersions on anyone else. Never say, "I deserve this more than (this or that fellow staff member) because . . . " Provide a concise statement of what you have achieved. It isn't bragging to be specific, and the more specific you can be, the better. For example, "Sales of our brand increased 18 percent in the last quarter, due to efforts and incentives I created, which were carried out by my department," or "Even though the two employees who left last year were not replaced, our productivity has not been affected, but rather has markedly increased due to the strategies I devised."

4. Poor-mouthing or whining is never attractive, certainly not when you want to take a step up the ladder. Never say you want *anything* from your employer because "my rent went up," "I don't feel I am being recognized," or "I need a new car." No boss wants to hear anyone's sad story, at least not

when asking for something. Remember, you are politely asking for the recognition you deserve, not for your begging bowl to be filled. I once worked with someone needy who had some issue or another regularly. One year, when bonus time was approaching, he went to his manager and told her he had already booked a vacation and arranged to have work done on his house. He wanted to be assured that his pre-bonus personal expenses would be covered! As the manager later said to me, "How is it my problem that he spent his bonus without knowing what it would be?" In addition to being an unprofessional thing to do since no one should ever let managers or other colleagues know they *need* money, it breached the most important two words in employee–employer relationships: *professional boundaries*.

5. Do not make up other offers. Saying that you have had several good job offers from competing companies as a hint that you might leave if your wishes aren't met is tantamount to asking someone to respond with, "I don't blame for you for considering those offers, and I will accept your resignation." The only time to use other offers as a ploy is when you are prepared to quit and have an offer nailed down, but aren't unhappy where you are and want to give the company a chance to retain you. If you are being interviewed for a job, you can mention that you are speaking to other companies or considering other offers, but don't push so hard that they think you're not specifically interested in their company. It never hurts to say, "You're my first choice right now," as that shows enthusiasm but still allows you the option of turning down an offer if one is made.

BE THE PERSON YOU WOULD WANT
ON YOUR TEAM

Some things never go out of style, and the Golden Rule is one of them. By all means, do unto others as you would have them do unto you. Whenever you see someone at work doing something you don't care for, think of your own actions and consider if that other person's behavior might occasionally be yours as well. It's easy to sneer at gossip or seethe when someone passes off your idea as their own, but when those occasions arise, look upon them as a reminder to review your own behavior.

Above all, be ethical. In today's slick business environment, that might seem like a gray area, but we all know it isn't. The truth is whispering softly in your heart, and you should always listen to it. If in doubt, ask someone you trust for their thoughts about any dilemma. Remember, that's what you want to be, too: a person whom others trust and look up to. In the words of the late Barbara Bush, "Never lose sight of the fact that the most important yardstick of your success will be how you treat other people—your family, friends, and coworkers, and even strangers you meet along the way."

A REFRESHER ON BASICS

Let's briefly look at some of the topics that I've discussed in other chapters, this time looking at them strictly as they apply to your work.

- Always dress for the job you want. Follow all the dress rules in chapter 1, but be extra-cautious. That means don't overdo the casual aspect of Casual Fridays. I've seen executives show up at meetings in baggy pants and slippers. Yes, slippers. The dress code being relaxed isn't the same as relaxing as if you were going to bed. A survey by the OfficeTeam staffing agency found that 80 percent of executives say clothing affects an employee's chance of being promoted.

- Dress with respect for yourself and others. For starters, wear clean clothing. How difficult is that? Difficult for some, judging by the odiferous crowds on elevators or public transport some days. Do you wear a uniform for your work that relieves you of the worry that people will know you have pulled on the same clothes as yesterday and the day before? You can't fool all the people all the time. Make sure your clothes aren't stained, wrinkled, or smelly.

- Dress simply yet stylishly, and apply this rule to hair, makeup, and accessories as well. No bedhead or tangled morning messiness, please. Clean hair and fresh makeup are a must. You don't want to look as if you were out bar-hopping, then raced home solely to refresh your Madly Magenta Iridescent Glow-in-the-Dark lipstick. In fact, you never want to seem as if you have been out on the town: the statement that might rock your world between 7 p.m. and midnight is not going to make the same impression at an early-morning meeting. Also, while a fitness room or office gym can be a great perk, you are still at work when using it. If your workout wear is too revealing, it could lead to your downfall, as in "out-of-work wear." At work, you are never invisible and are always being judged, not only on your performance but also on your wardrobe—its expense or even its fashionability aren't as important as how modest and suitable for the occasion your clothes are. If in doubt, check out chapter 1 again to get your closet organized and your act together.

- Organize your workspace. If your clothing choices speak volumes about you, your workspace whispers either "I'm a professional" or "Welcome to a microcosm of my disorganized mind." Whether you have a cubicle, office, or share a worktable, even if you are a hot-desker sitting at a different spot every day, keep it clean and orderly. Never decorate your space (or, if you have a job that provides a locker, the locker door, inside or out) as if it were your bedroom at home. That means no Bruno Mars posters, no stuffed animals, no framed sarcastic sayings. If you share workspace, clean up when you leave, so the next person using the space won't have to wipe it down.

- Be thoughtful about any shared space. That means saving your favorite spicy curries, salsas, and hot barbecue sauces for weekends and your heavy, musky colognes for nights out rather than stinking up the office. If you have a break room, do your part in keeping it clean. Don't ignore spilled coffee or a half-eaten sandwich just because neither is yours. Clean it up or take it to the trash bin. And wipe off surfaces when you have finished eating.

Do you telecommute? These rules apply to videoconferences as well. Remember, just as you can see them, they can see you.

VIDEO CONFERENCING ETIQUETTE

Even your video presence says everything about your brand and integrity.

1. If you're going to show up to a video conference call dressed in your suit or any business attire, make sure you're presentable head to toe! We often have to get up unexpectedly to answer the door, check on our children, or take the dog out. One way to handle this is to mute yourself before you walk away. Secondly, if you think you'll be disruptive to the other attendees, turn off your video and audio until you come back. This is about common courtesy and being respectful, which is earned through micro actions everyday.

2. If you have an office door and can close it, please do. That way you're preventing the possibility of distractions during your meeting.

3. Even when you're working remotely, those people who put in effort to get dressed for their video calls and their day in general feel better about themselves. I've been on plenty of calls with women who didn't plan to leave the house that day but were still rockin' their red lips.

4. Do not eat while you're on a video call. Sipping a tea or water occasionally is OK.

5. And finally, be present. Don't have your eyes on your cell phone or work on something else. It's telling others you don't care enough to pay attention, which will cost you respect. Remember, it's the micro actions that create our brand and earn us respect.

My last point is one I probably don't have to tell most of you, but it is so vital to your job security and success that I'm going to tell you anyhow. No matter how easy it might be to do so, never take supplies home. They are not there be filched. Whether it's a ream of paper, a flash drive, or a few pens, none of these are "perks" of any job. Taking them for personal use is theft. Besides being a grubby thing to do, cadging supplies is a fireable offense.

CREATING THE PROPER IMAGE

If the only people you hold in high regard and try to impress are those above you on the totem pole, you're doing it wrong. One of your coworkers or clients might be the person who could help you get or stand in the way of a promotion someday, but that isn't the only reason you should strive to treat everyone else with courtesy and respect. Showing respect for everyone with whom you come into contact is, in the eyes of employers, the heart of being a team player. Plus, you'll be more popular with coworkers and feel better about yourself. Seeing others as equals in your workplace also means staying home from work when you're sick. Nothing brings down productivity like spreading germs, and the sneezing, sniffling employee is more likely to get dirty looks than sympathy. If you work someplace where sick days are like gold nuggets and you can't afford to stay home with a cold, wear a mask to keep your germs from infecting colleagues. It's a good idea to keep a bottle of hand sanitizer at your desk or in your locker so that even when you feel in superb health, you can keep yourself from picking up someone else's germs and spreading them.

You can both show respect to others and help them advance by praising those who do good work and advocating for them. That's being professional. Trying to connect with them on social media or selling them anything, whether you're flogging raffle tickets for your kid's school fundraiser or pitching your CBD oil or whatever other multilevel marketing product you sell for extra spending money, disrespects personal boundaries and doesn't belong at work.

Mind your meeting manners. Be on time, always. You can control this with your own meetings by not scheduling anything back-to-back. Instead, leave five to ten minutes between them. Out of consideration for others, don't let your meetings run over the allotted time limit. When you attend a meeting in a conference room or share a group workstation, stay within your boundaries. Don't claim territorial rights by sprawling all over the place and spreading out your papers, pens, iPad, and whatever else you feel you need for work without considering the needs of others. And, not to nag, but will you please sit up straight? Yes, I understand that sitting at a desk or in meetings all day can be exhausting and hard on your spine. But I want you to succeed. So, sit up straight and keep your legs together (see the previous section on body language).

Not only is slouching hard on your back and bad for your posture, it also makes you look uninterested—and if there is one look that isn't good at work, not even if your supervisor is going on and on about her car problems, it is lack of interest. Speaking of not-so-great looks, if you are not wearing a top that tucks into trousers or a skirt, make sure the waistband isn't too low or the top too short when you sit down. Work is not a place to flash your body, no matter how hard you've worked at getting it into competitive shape.

For your own sake, make sure you stay hydrated and keep your circulation moving. If you don't wear some type of fitness band to remind yourself to move every hour, you can set a reminder on your phone. Just stand up and walk to the restroom or up and down a flight of stairs or, if you're alone, jog in place for a few minutes. You will have more energy as a result, and energetic is a good look for anyone.

There isn't a single suggestion in any other part of this book that shouldn't be followed at work. Good manners aren't a jacket to put on or take off whenever you please. Good manners are more like a second skin—they are with you all the time. Once learned, they will last you a lifetime, long after your other jackets have fallen to shreds or been deposited at a consignment shop.

"MANNERS EASILY MATURE INTO MORALITY."
—HORACE MANN

Be ambitious. Be determined. But always be respectful. And always work to inspire yourself as well as your colleagues. Your projects will not always be successful; your work might not be recognized as often as you wish. Still, part of your duty to yourself and the road to contentment lies in finding your happy place every day. Thoughtfulness toward coworkers will feed your positivity, as will celebrating all the small wins rather than postponing satisfaction until the big ones.

For most of us, a sizable portion of our lives is spent working. Treat that as a burden, and it will become one. Take pleasure in tasks, meetings, and the manner in which you handle difficult situations. Take pride in the respect of your colleagues and your good relationships with them. Your positivity will go a long way toward making sure you are recognized and rewarded. And you will find both fulfillment and peacefulness along the way.

CHAPTER 8

UNLEASHED AND IN THE OPEN

Don't Be a Lout When Out and About

If your parents were like mine, you probably heard the same admonishment when being sent or taken somewhere out of the house. Whether to a party, play, religious service, or even the neighborhood playground, the words were the same. "Be on your best behavior," we were told, knowing there was an "or else" unvoiced at the end. As adults, we have no one around to tell us that, but we shouldn't require politeness orders. In a perfect world, an adult's behavior would always be their best.

Unless you are a recluse or a hermit living a contemplative life in a cave, you have certainly noticed that when it comes to being on one's best behavior, many people—maybe even you—haven't fully grown up.

One good thing about being on one's best behavior is that it's easy. Show respect and consideration for other humans, and you will have succeeded. We've covered many aspects of first-class behavior already, so let's take a look at how we act when we're out and about, not necessarily doing anything special, but mixing among strangers.

> "KEEP YOUR THOUGHTS POSITIVE BECAUSE YOUR THOUGHTS
> BECOME YOUR WORDS. KEEP YOUR WORDS POSITIVE
> BECAUSE YOUR WORDS BECOME YOUR BEHAVIOR."
> —MAHATMA GANDHI

It's all about attitude, especially in public, where people judge you based on what they see. If your attitude is positive and you want other people to have as good a time as you are, you will tend to be at your best. This can also save you from bad moments. Let's say that rather than get into (or continue) an argument with your child, parent, or partner, you stomp out of the house to take a walk and cool down. If you think of that walk in terms of having left your bad attitude behind, you will certainly feel better faster. Try it sometime. Just smiling at people you pass on the street or enjoying the beauty of nature will make you feel better. Sometimes just going through the actions of feeling good will make you feel terrific. And being mindful of your environment as you walk will put you in *that* moment, not the previous angry one.

Remember when people were hooked on the whole *Pokémon Go* thing? It was a game, right? According to one analysis, the mobile game may have contributed to nearly 150,000 traffic accidents, 256 deaths, and economic costs of $2 billion to $7.3 billion in the first 148 days after its introduction to the US. People were so intent on finding tokens and winning points in the game that their eyes were glued to their phones and they were thinking only of *Pokémon Go*. Whether walking or driving, it's important to be mindful and aware of everyone who is affected by your actions. If, say, you're storming along in a funk, replaying an argument in your head and not aware of where you are at the moment, you aren't going to walk your way to a better mood, and you might accidentally knock someone down or purposefully elbow them out of the way. That someone might then take out your bad temper on someone else. No man or woman is an island—our rudeness can start an entire chain of events.

Yes, even in as minor an activity as walking around the block, you can be a force for good or not. Put yourself behind the wheel of a moving vehicle, and you can either ease people's way or be a downright danger.

IDIOT? OR MANIAC?

The late comedian George Carlin had a classic routine about how "anybody driving slower than you is an idiot, and anyone going faster than you is a maniac." We all have days when we feel that way, and we all have days when we ourselves are the ones driving like an idiot or a maniac. Either way, you might be putting others (and yourself) at risk along with making someone's good mood sink into the asphalt or their blood pressure skyrocket.

Driving is such a normal part of our day that we rarely stop to consider that we're in control of powerful machinery weighing two tons or more, while surrounded by other people who are in the same position. Safety as well as civility requires us to be alert and aware and not turn any drive into a no-holds-barred battle with other drivers.

You might be thinking, *I'm such a good driver, I could do it with my eyes closed.* But the police won't accept that as an excuse if you run a red light or pass a stop sign with only a rolling stop. And if you commit enough offenses, you will eventually lose your license. Whatever you do, smugness about one's driving skills is rarely rewarded.

Think about the worst things you've seen others doing while you're driving, the kind of actions that have made you mutter "Idiot!" Then ask yourself if you have been guilty of the same actions. People get killed every day reaching to pick up an object they've dropped on the floorboard or trying to find the preset button for their favorite station on the radio. Here's a little tip that will keep you safe: when you're driving, just drive, and do nothing else—nothing, *nada,* zip, zero.

Boss Vibes Driving Promises

I hereby promise that I will not:

- Tailgate another car
- Drive above the limit in a school zone
- Pass a stopped school bus from either direction if its red lights are flashing

- Cut off other drivers
- Race other drivers
- Lean on the horn
- Let my mind drift—because I know my eyes will follow
- Cut off a pedestrian who has the right of way (best never to cut off pedestrians, period)
- Jump or run a traffic light
- Drive dangerously slow on freeways or major highways, especially in the passing lane
- Shave or put on makeup
- Eat
- Try to read, text, look at a map or stare at the navigation screen, or (and, yes, I have seen it) watch videos
- Become lost in conversation with passengers to the point where you are on autopilot and not paying attention to the road
- Drive with bright lights on in traffic
- Make turns or change lanes without signaling

One wise safety measure when in your car is never to respond to an angry motorist who's yelling, breaking one of the above rules, or giving you a finger salute. At best, it will put you in as vile a mood. At worst, in these days of road rage, you could get hurt. Pushing your luck with aggressive drivers simply isn't worth the risk.

WORK OUT—BUT STAY IN YOUR LANE

Narcissists. Every gym and fitness club has them: members who have gone from fit to fanatical about working out and act as if the place were the private health spa in their mansion. They strut about as if no other members have paid as much to use the equipment for their physical and emotional health. It's important not to let these people get under your skin or ruin your workout routine. Equally important, you mustn't pick up any of their bad habits or treat others as if you deserved special rights. Note: you can avoid many issues simply by reading the gym rules.

Nothing shouts "narcissist" more than flaunting your birthday suit. The less you do it, the more people will feel comfortable around you. Ergo, keep your naughty bits to yourself. If you shower, pass between the locker room and the showers wrapped in a towel. Push yourself as much as you like during your fitness routine, but there is no gain in pushing the bounds of comfort for others. This is not a place for you to flaunt your confidence or indifference. It's about respecting the public space.

Fitness wear was created for specific functions—for example, yoga pants are designed so you will remain both comfortable and modest in any posture, even upside down, while running clothes are fashioned to keep you cool during a sweaty jog. You shouldn't be wearing anything not fit for your routine at the gym—for instance, baggy shorts in headstands are not a good idea. On the other hand, if you want to look cool and stylish, forget about showing up at any nonathletic event, be it Sunday brunch or a theatrical performance, in the apparel that fits in so well at 24 Hour Fitness.

I've found that most people in gyms are considerate and just want to get on with their workouts, watch the TVs up on the wall while they run or climb or pedal, and then get out. For the most part, politeness prevails, especially as good clubs and gyms are firm about not using the place as a phone booth for catching up on calls or a singles bar for hitting on other exercisers.

There are, however, several violations of etiquette I feel strongly about that are among the cardinal sins of gym users. The first is neglecting to clean a machine after you use it. For your own hygiene, I suggest cleaning before as well, because you can't rest assured the previous user did. This is not a difficult chore, since every gym has wipes and spray bottles close at hand and well-marked. If you do anything that makes you sweat profusely—running, lifting, steep cycling programs—make sure you don't inadvertently share your sweat every time you shake your head by keeping a towel around your neck or close by and wiping yourself down frequently.

Another sin is hogging the equipment. Once you have done your reps, don't "rest" on the machine. Step away and give someone else a chance, then come back to it. Maybe the episode of the house-hunting or renovate-and-grow-rich show on the screen above your machine has you hooked, but unless you're actively peddling, rowing, walking, or running, watch it from a different vantage point.

Speaking of equipment, treat it as if it were your own. That means don't drop weights, and put anything you've removed back in place when you're finished.

Lastly, respect everyone's personal space. Don't get too close, even if it's just with your yoga mat. Don't block the mirrors others are using to perfect their motions. Circuit training? Keep your circuit tight and circular, so people can easily figure out which equipment you're heading to next (and so you'll know which spots are free). When in doubt, ask. Graciousness demands that if someone comes up to you and starts giving you advice, you need to be polite, even if you're such a serious regular that you could be Gym Rat of the Year. Don't make the same mistake yourself, either; unless you work for the facility, your role doesn't include getting involved in someone else's regimen. There are trainers on hand if someone wants to be coached or corrected. Respect everyone's privacy and space.

The US has always been pretty relaxed in terms of formal etiquette rules, which can be a relief, but it has the downside of people acting as if everywhere they go is theirs. The gym is no one's rec room; it's a public facility. Accept that fact and the sensibilities of others, and you'll be working out your manners as well as your muscles.

PUBLIC SPACES ARE SHARED PLACES

Many of the previous chapters cover how we should act toward others, but again, even if rules aren't posted, there are rules that should not be broken when you're out and about if breaking them means infringing upon another person's pleasure.

One is in a theater of any kind. I can't fathom why anyone might think texting or reading messages and emails in the middle of a stage performance or movie doesn't count as using their cell phone only because it's silent. Not only is it annoying, it's also painful as the sudden brightness of your phone hits your neighbor's eyes—and even more unforgiveable at the theater, where sudden lights can make an actor forget lines or miss a cue. Lights, camera, action? Let's leave that at the movie set, not the movie theater.

Some common issues are now less of a problem due to the new recliner/stadium seating spreading across the States. If your movie is playing at a theater with old-style seating, don't battle with the person next to you for the armrest or put your feet up on the seat back in front of you. If you want to be more comfortable, watch DVDs or stream something at home.

One of the behavior patterns I see too often is people showing up late and irritating others. If you're constantly walking in when the theater is dark and something is flashing on the screen—even if it's an ad—you're late. A film can transport viewers to new worlds and other planets, but you will need to get to the theater first, park if you come by car, stand in the ticket line (unless there is preordering and ticket machines), and stand in line again to pick up snacks. Then there's that restroom stop and finding your seat. Leave plenty of time for all.

Also, since when are trailers not considered part of the movie-going experience? It's rare to go to the movies without some people chattering loudly and passing nachos back and forth during the coming attraction previews, making them difficult to watch and hear. This is not your living room; that cozy reclining seat is not in front of your large-screen TV. Like Mom said, be on your best behavior, which includes being on time, apologizing if you need to slide by seated patrons to take your seat, eating your popcorn or nachos as quietly as possible, depositing your trash in the receptacle by the door when you leave. The people paid to clean up the theaters after the screening aren't your servants.

The idea that the world is one big neighborhood coffeehouse where anything goes is now apparent in once-sacred spots like museums. It's hard to appreciate the art in some museums when you have to negotiate around a crowd of people who see a masterpiece solely as a backdrop for selfies. You see everything in museums these days: parents pushing screaming babies in strollers through the rooms; grown men and women crashing into each other as they experience everything through the lens of the phone they're using to view and video the exhibits; couples sitting on the viewing benches eating a snack or even making out; and a large percentage of the museum-goers speaking in everyday loudness levels about what they're seeing or even where they'll be lunching when they leave.

> "RUDENESS IS NOT HAVING FUN, AND IF IT IS, IT'S AT THE EXPENSE OF ANOTHER PERSON."
> —MARCO PIERRE WHITE

One place you're allowed—even encouraged—to eat and drink is at gallery openings, which fit more under the heading of "parties" than "cultural activities." Otherwise, be it at an exhibition, ballet, play, or opera, stay as silent as possible. If you come to a live performance and will need cough drops or hard candies for a dry throat, unwrap them before the show starts, because the crinkly sounds might as well be freight trains when picked up by a theater's acoustics. When you have something you absolutely must say, keep your voice low. And if you bring children with you (which you should not, other than to a children's matinee), bite the bullet and take them outside if they get rambunctious or start to wail.

Part of the pleasure of a shared experience requires not interfering with anyone else's enjoyment. That means not shouting at each other in restaurants, even in large groups, and being aware when you have had enough to drink that you risk being obnoxious. If someone in your group has crossed the line and is making a spectacle of themselves, be a responsible adult and tell them to cool it because they're embarrassing both of you, bumming out other people trying to have a good time, and working your nerves. If your entire group turns loud and rowdy, suggest moving on to the kind of bar meant for hearty partying.

Respect other diners and the staff in a restaurant by enjoying your food—and respecting them. This applies to fast-food joints as well as starched-linen dining establishments. Ordering at a counter doesn't give you the right to be uncivil. Show minimum-wage workers as much respect as you would show formal servers. From the food prep workers to the order takers, they're working hard for little money. Treating everyone considerately, even if they're not being especially considerate of you, will keep you calm. That will aid both your mood and your digestion. It will help customers in line after you get good treatment as well.

Here are a few fast-food suggestions. Get off to a good start by deciding what you want *before* you get in line so you don't keep others waiting. Spills and greasy dropped foods are a danger, so be sure to tell a staff member if you drop some fries or spill a drink so they can clean it up before someone slips and falls. Don't pocket the packets: restaurants are to eat in, not a loading zone for stocking up on sweetener, straws, napkins, or condiments. Put your trash and tray where they belong when you're finished eating.

The takeaway here isn't a bag of burgers—it's a gentle reminder that as long as you're aware of others and courteous toward them in any locale or environment, whether you're at the movies, grabbing a quick bite, climbing to nowhere on a stair stepper, or behind the wheel of a car, you will feel more positive about life and pass on positivity to others.

CHAPTER 9

BON VOYAGE!

Minding Your Manners on the Go

Whether you're an eager adventurer or a reluctant voyager, travel is stressful. Yes, we can get places faster than ever thanks to planes and high-speed trains and more people overseas speak English than they used to, but travel in the twenty-first century can be more challenging than ever before. Everyone has horror stories to share. Still, travel can't be avoided, and for those who want to experience the world, it must be embraced. Think of all the wonderful people you've met and all the soulful connections you've made because you chose to travel.

I want to help you make your journeys more manageable for yourself and those around you.

If you truly dislike traveling, it's important to psych yourself up before you head out your own front door. Use the internet or a guidebook to get acquainted with the place or places you will be going to. Mark the pages or make notes on anything that you will need to know quickly: for example, numbers to call in an emergency, public transport and taxi information at your destination, currency exchange information, airport information if you will be changing planes.

Make sure each piece of your luggage has an ID tag on it, and double-check that anything you might require in transit is in your carry-on. Even if you're traveling by bus or train, you won't always be able to get to your other bags or have space in which to open them. Don't forget to weigh your bags after packing. Most airlines now have either size or weight limitations for checked and on-board bags, and you will pay heavily for every extra pound. Look on individual company websites for exact weights, dimensions, and possible fees.

THE PLANE TRUTH

As a frequent flyer, both nationally and internationally, I know that one of the most stressful parts of travel can be the period before boarding. We have to be at the airport hours before our departure time, for starters. When we arrive, we may discover that our flight has been delayed. The lucky ones are those departing from airports that have coffee bars and shops located before the security area, because if you will be sitting in an airport for hours, it's nice to have a change of venue for browsing or hanging out while you're there. Otherwise, once you have checked in, there's nowhere to go but through security.

"I HAD ARRIVED AT THE AIRPORT . . . EARLY SO
THAT, IN ACCORDANCE WITH AIRLINE PROCEDURES,
I COULD STAND AROUND."

—DAVE BARRY

Check-in, other than occasionally long waits, is rarely stressful, unless your flight has been cancelled or your bag is overweight. In most cases, if there's a problem with delays, ticketing, or baggage requirements, the check-in agents can handle it. Then you're off to security, with your handbag or briefcase and your carry-on bag, having already verified from home if you are allowed to bring two separate items on board with you. Smaller airlines, especially overseas, might allow only one piece for free, in which case, if you cram the smaller item into the larger, you might need to take your purse or attaché onto the plane and check that carry-on bag.

Preplanning is the key to both a flawless check-in experience and a smooth passage through security. If you aren't enrolled in TSA PreCheck or Global Entry, you will want to make sure that (1) your cell phone and all other electronic devices are easily available and ready for screening, (2) any liquids and creams are under maximum size and already inside a one-quart zip-style clear plastic bag, and (3) your shoes can be easily removed. When you get to the bin area, you don't want to be holding up the line, so in addition to the three points listed above, you won't want to get in line wearing unnecessary items that need removing. That means no chunky jewelry, no belts containing metal, nothing at all that's complicated to remove, and removing your jacket and scarf before you reach the front of the line. Your mission here is to get everything that needs to be there into the bins as quickly as possible to keep the line moving. And don't forget to check for water! Many a line has been held up due to small water bottles forgotten in bags. If you are determined to wear all your accessories while traveling, it's best to keep them in your purse or briefcase so that once you pass security, you can put them on.

Either the central area, where the gates converge, or the gate areas themselves, usually have one or two fast-food or regular restaurants and bars. These are not waiting rooms, and if you want to use them you need to be prepared to pay heavily for whatever you consume. And, yes, it's a shame we all have to chug our water before we pass through security, but you're allowed to take your empty bottle through and fill it up from taps once you're free of security, so you aren't forced to pay the exorbitant prices at the shops or bars. Most airports have special filtered water taps specifically for people who travel with their own water bottles. But the restaurants are for customers only. If you do choose to grab a bite, put your carry-on under the table, out of the way, so no one will trip on it. Do not place it on an empty seat. Regardless of how many are in your party, your purchase provides you with only one seat per person.

Once you get to the gate, the same rule applies: you get a seat, but your baggage does not, unless another is unquestionably free and unneeded. If the waiting area is crowded, don't think you're fooling anyone if you stash your backpack on the seat next to you, then gaze off in a different direction as if the seat is someone else's being saved. If anyone boarding after you looks longingly at the seat, don't make them beg. Smile and shift your bag to the floor beneath the seat in front of you.

Every time I travel—and believe me, I'm never looking for things to go wrong or seeking inappropriate behavior—I always come across someone doing something bizarre. I once saw a lady combing her hair as she was standing in line on the jet bridge. Let's not do anything while we're on the jet bridge except smile, greet our neighbors in line if appropriate, and be patient as we board the plane.

Sometimes the bridge and plane are securely overlapped, but at others, there's a gap between the two. I once chatted with a flight attendant as I was walking onto the plane, and she noted that many phones slip and fall to the tarmac because the people boarding are not paying attention. It takes less than five minutes between the time you scan your boarding pass to the moment you step onto the plane. Surely you can stay off your phone long enough to avoid the risk of making your trip without one.

If boarding is on a first-come, first-served basis, as is common on some budget airlines, get there early and be prepared to stand if you want to board first. Never try to sneak into the line just because you weren't willing to get there earlier or pay an early boarding fee. If you're choosy about where you sit or how much you can carry on (some airlines will let you fly with a carry-on plus your handbag or attaché while others make you pay a tariff for the privilege), check the rules and pay in advance, as it will cost more to add anything extra to your ticket at the airport. The "plane truth" is that making your departure easier is possible if you're willing to spend a bit more time or money.

THE GOOD NEIGHBOR POLICY

When you fly, unless it's a puddle-jumper or some friend's private jet (wishful thinking on my part), you will usually be one of 85 (Boeing 737) to 525 (Airbus A380) people in a confined space. Courtesy demands making an effort so your mere presence won't offend anyone. That might sound self-evident, but if you have ever been on a long-haul flight next to someone reeking of body odor or heavy perfume, you know that this is a rule many don't follow. Make sure your hair has been washed and that you're wearing clothing that's both comfortable and clean. A few dress code rules are wise to follow: no muscle shirts with armpit hair sticking out, no short-shorts or tight Spandex pants, no sandals with less than pristine feet. This is an airplane, not a beach or a shower room. Just covering your armpits isn't enough—you also want to make sure they don't smell like a sewer. There's no excuse for not wearing deodorant—even if you follow a vegan or organic lifestyle, there are plenty of natural, nontoxic sweat-stoppers available. In the bad odors department, if you are bringing any of your own food onto a plane to eat midflight, make sure it's not smelly. In recirculated air, it could trigger the gag reflex of someone nearby. If you really need a slice of spicy pizza or a burger with everything on it, eat it before you board, then brush your teeth. If you get to the airport early, you won't be rushed.

As you get on board, it's polite to help others who might be struggling to place a bag in the overhead bin. But don't feel obliged unless you're tall and relatively strong. If it's open seating, don't dawdle, and if the attendants tell you to go to the back of the plane, do so. When you have an aisle or middle seat and the window seat isn't yet occupied, I suggest that you don't fasten your seat belt until the row has filled. If someone wants the seat, rise graciously to let them in. When it's open seating, you can feel free to set your purse or book on the middle seat if it's unoccupied, but if someone asks if the seat is free, the only suitable answer is to smile, nod, and remove your belongings.

"THE JOURNEY NOT THE ARRIVAL MATTERS."
—UNKNOWN

Once seated, here are a few general suggestions to make the trip hassle-free, for yourself as well as for other passengers.

- Yes, your seat goes back, but that doesn't mean it needs to. With so little space between rows, courtesy counts, and it's polite to keep the angle of your recline slight. In particular, don't put your seat back during food or beverage service, since it makes it difficult or even impossible for the person behind you to move freely.

- Unless you have boarded some kind of chartered party plane, good manners require never acting as if you're on one. What you're on is a metal tube in the sky conveying preoccupied people from one place to another, a process few other than children find exciting. While you might be wide awake and raring to go, some of those sharing your space might be on their third connection of the day, anxious flyers, or on the way home from a long trip and already suffering from jet lag.

- The well-mannered flyer is one who doesn't speak loudly to a companion, especially one seated across the aisle, and who respects others' desire to sleep.

- Seats are narrower than ever, which makes it imperative to respect boundaries. Fighting your neighbor for the armrest or using the floor area by your seat as a trash bin won't make the trip better. No one wants to wade through a sea of plastic bags, electronics, and newspapers just to get to the restroom. This is especially important on long-haul flights, where I've seen passengers trying to disembark while slipping on plastic blanket bags and tripping on crumpled blankets that have made their way into the main aisles.

- When you use the restroom, be conscious that other people will want to use it after you. Leave it as clean as possible. I suggest following the requests that used to be posted in every lavatory: let the flight attendant know if any items need replacing and wipe down the sink before you exit.

- If you don't want to talk to the chatty person in the seat next to you, you can try the earbud escape and listen to music, make it very obvious you're deeply enjoying a book or magazine, sleep, or pull out your electronic device and work.

- Flight attendants are not always committed to making the skies friendly. Some aren't happy in their work and take it out on travelers, being super inattentive or snarky, as if any request is an imposition. On the other hand, flight attendants have to deal with rude, demanding passengers all the time, so it's thoughtful to treat them with courtesy and appreciation. They are not, as Paul Westerberg sang, waitresses in the sky. They are there for your safety, not as anyone's servants. Try to stay out of their way by not standing in the aisles or deciding the best time to use the restroom is when they're inching their way along with a beverage cart.

- Relax and enjoy the flight as much as you can. Keeping yourself in a positive frame of mind is vital to enjoying your journey and making it painless. This all comes down to respecting the boundaries of the shared space and behaving appropriately. We've all read, heard of, or witnessed bizarre behavior on planes ranging from clipping toenails to filing fingernails to flossing teeth while seated. No one wants to share their space with anyone else's nail clippings, nail dust, or debris from their last meal. (This is where that mask mentioned below comes in handy.) If someone is annoying you or behaving inappropriately, it's best to tell the flight attendants if you have asked nicely once.

One last note on flying is that it's wise to wear a mask on any flight. Under any circumstances, it's better to be safe than sorry. I also depend on a mask to filter out any foul smells that often spread during a flight. I put a drop of peppermint, lavender, or eucalyptus oil on the inside of the mask so that whenever a bad odor drifts my way, I can just breathe deeply and get a breath of fresh air, along with a relaxing scent.

Because travel, especially flying, is an anxiety-provoking experience for many, you can help others relax. If you're anxious

yourself, you will cope better by preparing. Here are some ideas
you might find helpful.

HELP AN ANXIOUS TRAVELER	KEEP CALM YOURSELF
Make small talk and ask about their trip.	Learn meditation or relaxation techniques.
Compliments share positivity. Give them, if possible, remembering that being genuine is key.	Keep something comforting close to you: a soft wool scarf or shawl, a baby pillow with a silk case, a cashmere or silk sleep mask.
Ask questions about their plans if a vacation trip or their work if it's for business.	Talk a little about your trip, where and why you're going, your plans.
Ask for help in choosing a movie to watch.	Watch a film—comedies are good if you're having difficulty concentrating.
Offer to share any magazines you have brought on board.	Bring along your favorite music or light reading: a favorite book to reread, magazines.

Although train travel tends to provoke less anxiety than fly-
ing, the above rules still apply—with one addition, and that
concerns the ubiquitous cell phone. If you must make a call
from your seat, keep your voice low or, when possible, go to the
end of the car (some trains have a soundproof booth in each car
specifically for phone calls).

Personally, I find train travel relaxing in itself—the rock-
ing motion and the scenery flashing by are so soothing that
the last thing I would choose to do is catch up on calls, but I

understand that making a call can be a necessity. Still, the only sound most people want to hear on a train is clackety-clack and not yakety-yak.

FARTHER AFIELD

I have traveled extensively, throughout the United States and internationally, for both business and pleasure. I have three key words to ensure a more pleasant trip: Prepare. Adapt. Respect.

Wherever you go, for whatever reason, it's always wise to read up on the city—and country, if you're going abroad—first. Knowing about the destination will make your trip more pleasurable because you will have familiarized yourself with the ins and outs of public transportation, tempting restaurants, don't-miss sights, and cultural options. Even if the trip is strictly business, it's usually possible to find the time to visit one notable landmark or enjoy a meal away from your hotel.

In any hotel, whether you're staying in a luxurious suite on an expense-paid business trip, in a chain hotel, or in an Airbnb, you are a *paying* guest, yes, but you are still expected to behave as a well-mannered one. Not doing so—noisiness late at night, running and shouting in the halls, smoking in nonsmoking areas—can end in having to find another place to stay. Being a good guest makes everyone's life easier.

It's a lovely treat having someone else tidying up your quarters and making the bed every day. Hotel cleaners are not highly paid, so tipping is always appreciated, as is being thoughtful and not making extra work for anyone. That means putting any trash in the wastebaskets, turning out the lights when you leave the room, and putting towels you don't plan to use again on the side of or in the empty bathtub to indicate that you'd like fresh ones. Many hotels now post signs asking that you help save water by using your towels for more than one day, and direct you to hang the towels on the towel racks to let them know you don't need a change.

Visiting foreign countries for the first time is daunting for most of us, so it's extra important to do some research and planning first. Here's a quick rundown that will make your travels in any country more enjoyable.

1. If English isn't spoken, learn the words for "Hello," "Please," "Thank you," and "Excuse me," as well as the phrase, "Do you speak English?" I had heard about how much French people disliked American visitors due to their sense of entitlement and lack of interest in learning about the language and culture while visiting, so when I was prepping for my first trip to Paris, I was nervous. I had taken a few years of French in high school, but I couldn't remember anything beyond a few greetings and words for some animals. This was before the days of Duolingo and Rosetta Stone, so I found a local school that taught the basics of conversational French. I went to just a few classes to learn how to get a cab, order food, and ask for basic help if needed. (Of course, now translation engines can do all that for you, along with all the apps that help you pronounce words correctly, but nothing beats actually learning some words.) During my travels, I was delighted to find that in every store I walked into, the staff appreciated being greeted in French even though I couldn't get past *"Je vais bien, merci. Comment allez-vous?"* Many would even teach me an extra phrase or two. I have

done this in many countries I've visited and noticed the increase in warmth and welcome when I use just a few words. It's a respectful way of showing that I appreciate the country I'm visiting.

2. If you are complaining about something in a foreign country, be sure your complaint (or request) is legitimate and courteous. Try to ask a question rather than lodge a complaint when possible. For example, ask "Are rooms always made up late or can I can request that mine by serviced in the mornings?" Well-meaning Americans can come off as abrupt and demanding in countries where the culture takes manners seriously. Sadly, some Americans start off their complaints in hotels or restaurants with "In America, we would never . . ." or "Why can't you people . . . ?" This is especially rude and resented.

3. Do your research and travel with notes, maps, and a good guidebook, either as paper copies or saved websites. Before you leave, you'll want to know the currency exchange rates and best ways to obtain cash (the best rate for transactions is usually obtained with your bank card at ATMs). Not familiarizing yourself with the local currency takes up other people's time at the supermarket or other shops, while not knowing traditional store hours can waste a lot of your own. For instance, in small towns in Europe, everything is closed on Sunday with the exception of restaurants, and some shops are closed until 4 p.m. on Monday.

4. Don't stick out by being dressed in a look that doesn't impress (and can offend) foreigners, who tend to be more conservative

and better dressed. That means no Lycra bicycle shorts or yoga pants on the street, no T-shirts or sweatshirts with four-letter words on them, and no workout shorts outside a fitness room.

5. Depend on research for acquainting yourself with cultural rules, so you won't be shunned for rudeness. For instance, in Thailand, when seated, your feet should not be pointing at anyone but crossed at the ankle and tucked beneath your chair. In temples, be prepared to remove your shoes before entering out of respect; the same goes for homes, hotel rooms, and small shops for reasons of cleanliness.

6. Most people know that life in other countries is not the same as life in the United States. It's your job to adapt. Avoid talking politics unless you're an expert on their country as well as our own and try not to judge anything by American standards. Remember, travel is an opportunity for learning, not for instructing.

7. Be sure to check the tipping rules for any country. Many Americans don't realize that in some countries, the service charge added to the bill goes to management. In some small towns, and, indeed, in some countries, tipping is not a thing and is even considered rude. In some nations, a 10 percent tip is the norm while in others, just leaving the equivalent of a dollar per person is appreciated.

"TRAVEL MAKES ONE MODEST. YOU SEE WHAT A TINY PLACE YOU OCCUPY IN THE WORLD."
—GUSTAVE FLAUBERT

The key to being a happy traveler is, as always, mindfulness and consideration. Travel truly does broaden the mind. It should be an invigorating, adventurous break from everyday life. Experiencing and enjoying a different culture is a humbling and enlightening adventure that forces us to re-examine long-held beliefs and reminds us that while other nationalities live differently than we do, we are all joined by our basic humanity.

CONCLUSION

THE SECRET

It's Now Yours, to Share or Not

Congratulations! You are now in possession of all the advice you will ever need to be confident and self-assured no matter the situation. As you've seen, you don't need to do any heavy lifting or make any major life changes in order to gain the respect of others and the benefits that come with that.

I'm hoping you have found your personal secret to becoming a better, happier you. The truth is there is no real secret, except to cultivate common sense and mindfulness in everything you do. We share this crowded planet with all sorts of people, some much like ourselves, some dissimilar. What we all have in common is our desire to get through each day and every experience with the most ease and least stress possible. That's where etiquette comes in.

You're in control here. You get to pick and choose. There is nothing in this book that could in any way hold you back from success, self esteem, and your ultimate Boss Vibes. Sure, in some areas—table manners, perhaps, or how you act in work meetings—you will need to be more conscious of your words and actions than ever before, but you will see immediate rewards in how others treat you and how you feel at the end of the day.

I suggest keeping this book handy, even highlighting areas in which you think you need all the help you can get. Work on both your strong points and your weak points. Make adjustments to your dress, your voice levels, how much you help others at work, your attentiveness when others are speaking, and be mindful not only of your own actions but of the effect they have on others. Week by week, you should sense an increase in the pleasant sensation of feeling better about yourself.

I know you can do this on your own—after all, people have been improving themselves ever since hunters and gathers learned to work together for their mutual benefit. The story of civilization is always a story of manners. It wasn't just beauty that tamed the beast; etiquette played a leading role.

I will close with a few last thoughts of what we've talked about and how you can excel in every area. I hope in our time together you have been able to take a good look at yourself and change anything in your dress, attitude, or behaviors that might be holding you back from the success and contentment you seek.

I suspect you know enough by now that you aren't in desperate need of the list below even if you were when you turned the first page. Regardless, this list is good to keep as you make your way through the world as a person exuding self-esteem and courtesy.

1. **Dress for the occasion.** Always appear professional at work. This is not the place where you want to stand out for your fashion daring. Keep in mind that there are parts of your body best exposed only to significant others and medical professionals.

2. **Perfect the fine art of listening.** That means showing interest, making eye contact, not fidgeting, and refraining from interrupting. Speak up so no one needs to strain in order to hear, but don't shout.

3. **Be the master or mistress of basic courtesies.** The more you show your respect for others, the more it will come back to you twofold.

4. **Keep yourself to yourself in terms of your physical being.** No one wants to hear, see, or sniff anything that belongs to the very private you.

5. **Stay flexible but know the rules.** No one is ever too young or too old to work on bettering their behavior. The rules change over time, but the underlying belief in thoughtfulness and consideration doesn't.

6. **Eat as if you're dining with the Queen—even when you're alone.** Table manners are one of the things that separate us from farm animals. Nowadays we have to eat so often on the run that we should take pleasure in dining in as fine a fashion as possible even if it's only takeout or fast food.

7. **Work rules are some of the most important you will ever have.** This isn't just because proper work etiquette is one of the keys to getting ahead (it is), but because it affects

everything you do. So much of your time is spent at your workplace that your manners there will always carry over to your life outside of work.

8. **Don't enjoy yourself in public at the expense of others.** Mindfulness means always being aware of those around you wherever you are. Whether on public transportation, dining out, at the gym, or at the movies, anytime there are other people present, it simply isn't all about you.

9. **The world is your oyster to be savored, not slurped.** Be a good traveler by being gracious. Do whatever you can to reduce stress when trapped in the confined space of planes, trains, and buses with total strangers for what might be hours on end. Remember, the skies are only as friendly as the people being flown through them.

If you can keep these points in mind, you have gotten the grip on etiquette you need to improve your life and make the world a happier place. It doesn't take much most of the time. Something as small as a smile can brighten a stranger's life. On the other hand, it doesn't take a whole lot to stir up anxiety, irritation, or anger in others or to take a high-speed elevator down to the basement of another's opinion or impression of you.

You can do it! As I mentioned in a previous example, think of how Melissa McCarthy's character changed and became a happier person by acting nice toward the end of *Identity Theft*. She experienced authenticity and friendship from these changes, things she never possessed while she was busy being defensive and inconsiderate for the majority of the movie. I would bet that just from a single reading of this book, you are already being more considerate toward others and feeling better about yourself and your life. As long as you start every day by reminding yourself to present your best self to the world, you will automatically be genuinely, thoughtfully, and noticeably more polite. The bonus will then be yours to reap: more confidence, success, and self-esteem forever!

ABOUT THE AUTHOR

Nita Patel is a speaker, author, and artist who believes in modern etiquette as a path to becoming our best selves. Schooled in London and a veteran of corporate America, she has 20+ years in technology and healthcare leadership and in nurturing teams toward confidence and impact. She is currently pursuing studies in psychology at Harvard while exploring the intersection of mindfulness and manners, empowering people to discover self-confidence and success through the lost art of etiquette. For more, visit Nita-Patel.com.

AUTHOR'S NOTE

For additional resources on how you can live your best life through the art of etiquette and more, visit nita-patel.com and drop me a note. See you there!